Spanish Military Jets 1954–2022

Difficult Beginnings

Volume 1

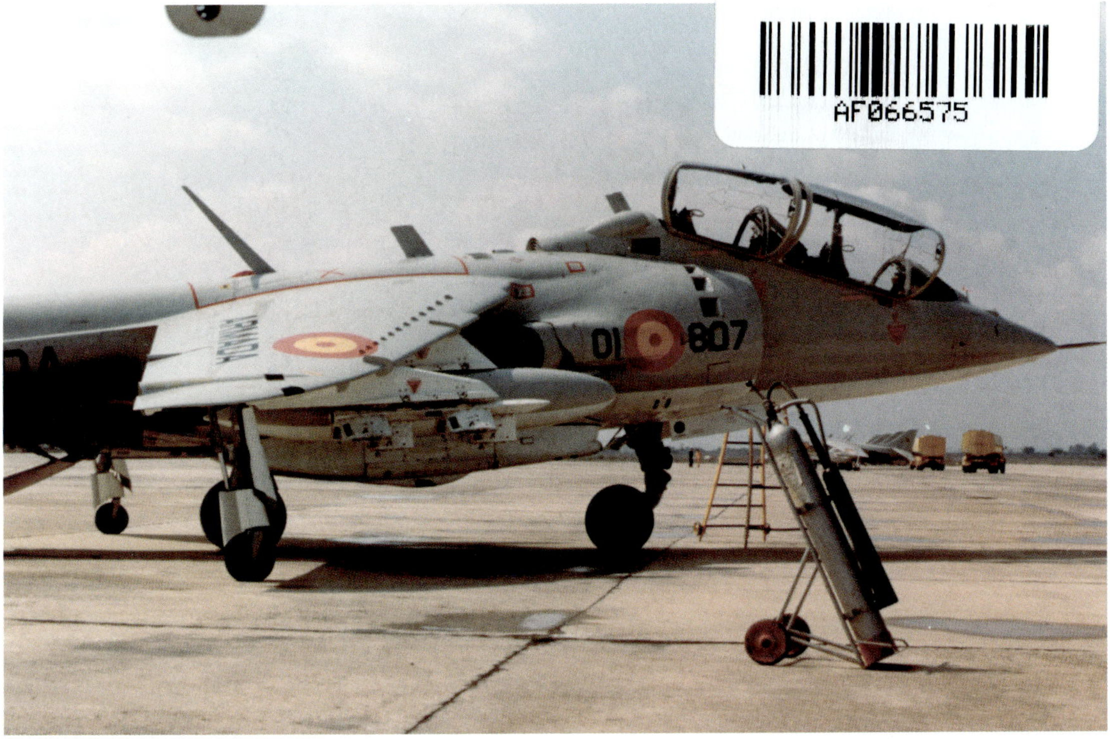

EDUARDO MANUEL GIL MARTÍNEZ AND
JUAN ARRÁEZ CERDÁ

KEY Books

MODERN MILITARY AIRCRAFT SERIES, VOLUME 9

Front cover image: An F-5M from Ala 23 waiting for its next flight. This aircraft is intended for advanced training to the new jet pilots within the EdA.

Back cover image: The prototype of the first Spanish-made jet: Hispano Aviación HA-200 Saeta. The aircraft is parked at San Pablo airport (Seville), waiting for a demo flight.

Title page image: Since its arrival, the AV-8S has been the main aircraft of the Spanish Navy. After several years, this aircraft type was replaced by the improved AV-8B.

Contents page image: Several aircraft were deployed to the Canary Islands on air defence duties. One of these aircraft was the Mirage F-1EE, like the one in the picture, which were deployed to Escuadrón 462 from Ala 46.

A Solete, mi vida.
A mis padres, Salud y Eduardo.
A Caco, Iñigo, Ibón y June.
A Merce y Ricardo.
A mis abuelos Mercedes, Salud, Mami, Manuel y Juan.

Published by Key Books
An imprint of Key Publishing Ltd
PO Box 100
Stamford
Lincs PE19 1XQ

www.keypublishing.com

The rights of Eduardo Manuel Gil Martínez and Juan Arráez Cerdá to be identified as the author of this book has been asserted in accordance with the Copyright, Designs and Patents Act 1988 Sections 77 and 78.

Acknowledgements
From Eduardo: Marisol García Gómez, Ricardo Ramallo Gil, José Antonio Muñoz Molero, the Ejército del Aire and José Luis González.

From Juan: A mis compañeros de la Hermandad de la Legión, a quienes cada día les gusta más nuestra Historia Aeronáutica Militar.

The photos used belong primarily to the Juan Arráez collection, and the sources of all others are listed in the photos caption.

Copyright © Eduardo Manuel Gil Martínez and Juan Arráez Cerdá, 2022

ISBN 978 1 80282 435 3

All rights reserved. Reproduction in whole or in part in any form whatsoever or by any means is strictly prohibited without the prior permission of the Publisher.

Typeset by SJmagic DESIGN SERVICES, India.

Contents

Foreword 4

Chapter 1	Lockheed T-33	7
Chapter 2	North American F-86 Sabre	14
Chapter 3	HA-200 Saeta and HA-220 Súper Saeta	23
Chapter 4	Lockheed F-104G Starfighter	34
Chapter 5	Dassault Mirage III	43
Chapter 6	Northrop F-5	55
Chapter 7	McDonnell Douglas F-4C Phantom	66
Chapter 8	Mirage F-1	73
Chapter 9	Harrier AV-8S	83
Chapter 10	EdA Structure and Radio Codenames	91

Glossary 94
Bibliography 95

Foreword

At the end of World War Two, the Spanish government realised that, despite having remained neutral, the victorious countries were beginning to withdraw their ambassadors and blocking trade with the Spanish nation, preventing the arrival of fuel and raw materials, such as tungsten. However, the country overcame these pressures, and, with the help of Argentina and other Latin American countries, began to recover little by little. It did not take long for the ambassadors who had left to return to Spain, and in December 1955, the UN recognised Spain as a fully-fledged member.

The Fuerzas Armadas de España (Spanish Armed Forces) had a large number of aircraft within it and a significant amount left over from the last civil war (1936–39), but the vast majority of the fleet was already very outdated.

Slowly, relations with European countries began to improve, especially with Germany, Italy and France, with whom agreements were signed, but not with Great Britain, although the relations were civil.

Faced with the belligerent attitude of the United Socialist Soviet Republic (more commonly known as the USSR), the United States approached Spain in 1953, reaching a Defence and Mutual Aid Agreement by which the Torrejón, Morón and Zaragoza Air Bases (AB) were built, as well as Base Naval de Rota (Rota Naval Base). Likewise, a series of radar bases that covered the entirety of the country were constructed. At all these bases, only the Spanish flag waved, as a sign of sovereignty. In addition, the issue of surveillance and security was the responsibility of the Spanish government.

A good part of my service with the Air Force was in the Alert and Control Squadron No. 5 at the Base Militar Aitana, which we shared with the 876th Aircraft Control and Warning Squadron of the United States Air Force (USAF). In 1953, Ejército del Aire (EdA, Spanish Air Force) was equipped with several dozen Messerschmitt Bf 109B and E veterans from the Spanish Civil War and just over a dozen Bf 109F.2s acquired from Germany during World War Two. There were also a few Polikarpov I-15bis aircraft that had been captured from the Republicans at the end of the Spanish Civil War.

The EdA decided to modernise itself, and, with American help, an air base was built in Talavera la Real, where the Escuela de Reactores (Jet School) was created and equipped with the Lockheed T-33A. Before that, a good number of pilots, both lieutenants, who had recently graduated from the Academia General del Aire (General Air Academy), and veteran officers and chiefs with a lot of flight experience, either went to the United States to train as jet pilots and fly the T-33 and the F-86F or to the American base in Furstelfenbruck, Germany.

On the afternoon of 30 June 1955, the first two Sabres assigned to the EdA from the United States Air Forces in Europe (USAFE) landed at Getafe AB. They came from Landstuhl Air Base (AB), which was later merged with Ramstein AB (Germany), taking its name, where the 86th Fighter Bomber Wing (FBW) was based (the unit that gave some of its aircraft to Spain). The Sabres USAF serial numbers were 51-13194 and 51-13239. They were reregistered by the EdA as C.5-1 and C.5-2, although the first one only served as a stationary training aircraft at the Escuela de Especialistas de León (Leon Base Specialist School).

The next delivery, which comprised five aircraft, occurred on 14 September 1955. They took off from the Chateauroux AB, France, and the American pilots who flew them belonged to the 527th Fighter Day Squadron (FDS, at the disposal of 86th FBW), of which the five aircraft had been decommissioned.

The rest of the Sabres arrived in batches between 1955 and 1959. The delivery flights primarily took place from the warehouse that the USAF owned at RAF Prestwick, Scotland, although on some occasions the aircraft also came from Chateauroux or Toul.

The EdA received a total of 270 aircraft from the US, which were distributed as follows: 18 F-86F-20s, 155 F-86F-25s, 32 F-86F-30s and 65 F-86F-40s. With them, several Alas de Caza (Fighter Wings) were created at the Spanish-American bases, but before that, the No. 1 Fighter Wing was born at Manises AB, to which, on 4 April 1959, the Combat Flag (Bandera de Combate) was delivered. Also, the new unit received the war trophies and Combat Diary of the Combat Group of the laureate Commander Joaquín García Morato, who had been the top 'ace' of the National Fighter branch (with 40 confirmed victories) during the Spanish Civil War. The No. 1 Fighter Wing, in which I had the honour of being stationed with in 1961, is the heir of the spirit of Morato's Combat Group, as well as upholding its traditions and its emblem and motto. I have many pleasant memories from my time in Manises, both from the trips to bases in France, Italy and Germany and from the visits of units from these countries to Manises. Although Spain was not a NATO member at this time, it maintained bilateral collaboration agreements with the organisation.

In 1951, taking advantage of a visit to Spain by Professor Willy Messerschmitt, the heads of the Hispano Aviación factory convinced him, given his inability to design and manufacture aircraft in Germany, to sign a two-year (extendable) contract to develop a twin jet for Escuela y as alto (School and Assault), which was named the HA-200 Saeta. Consequently, the German engineers Kraus, Hournung, Madelung, Ebner, Blümm, Clages, Cedulding, Hoffmann, Binz, Nerud, Schaefer and Klotz joined the project office, joining the Spanish team of José María Cerdeño, Ángel Figueroa, Rafael Rubio and Jaime Esteva Salom. The first Saeta flight took place on 12 August 1955. It was flown by test pilot Fernando de Juan Valiente. In total, 90 Saetas were manufactured, followed later by 25 copies of the HA-220 Súper Saeta attack single-seater version.

In 1959, the United Arab Republic (UAR, the ultimately failed merger of Egypt and Syria that lasted from 1958 until 1971) signed a contract with Hispano Aviación for the acquisition of the HA-200 manufacturing license plus ten aircraft, five flight-ready and five in pieces, as well as the necessary tools for its chain manufacturing. In 1960, on 21 June, the first five aircraft, with their wings removed and properly packed, landed at Factory No. 35 located at the Elwan AB, together with a small group of technicians under the command of Jaime Esteva Salom. Soon, Esteva Salom began the training of several Egyptian pilots while assembly was taking place, with the first aircraft already painted in the colours of the UAR. On 7 July, five aircraft took off for a demonstration during the military parade celebrating the eighth anniversary of their revolution before President Nasser, who was in attendance. There was an extensive advertising campaign in the press and radio, but what they never said was that the aircraft were Spanish, and that the pilot who impressed them most during the training was also Spanish and of Jewish ancestry.

Finally, the chain manufacturing began in the UAR, but when only a small number were flight-ready, a surprise attack by the Israeli Air Force, known as the Six-Day War, was launched. The attack managed to almost completely destroy Factory No. 35, the Saetas and other aircraft that were on its platform. And so, just like that, the story of the Egyptian Saetas ended, and the Spanish technicians were evacuated and sent back to Spain.

(There was another project sold to the UAR: the HA-300, a supersonic delta wing fighter of which only the prototype was manufactured, which is currently kept in the Oberschleissheim Museum in Germany.)

When CASA absorbed Hispano Aviación, it found in one of its project departments, a design that turned out to be of considerable interest. Its development was continued, and the CASA C-101 was created, an excellent training aircraft that is still in service, although sadly not for much longer. Not only was it successful in Spain, but also in Chile, which has 73, 23 of which were built there. Jordan acquired 16, and Honduras bought four.

Today, Spanish manufacturers participate in the most significant aerospace projects of the European community, such as the Eurofighter interceptor and the A400 transport.

Juan Arráez Cerdá
4 September 2021

A T-33 warming the engines at Zaragoza Air Base (AB). From 1973, all the T-33s left Talavera AB and joined Zaragoza AB (with Ala 41).

Chapter 1
Lockheed T-33

History

In the mid-to-late 1940s, Spain was in a very difficult situation; it was dealing with the hard task of rebuilding the country after the Spanish Civil War and the general shortage it was suffering due to international isolation and economic blockade following World War Two.

Faced with the inability to keep the aircraft that had been used until the end of World War Two operational, the Ministry of Air decided that the roughly 30 remaining Bf 109s should be kept in service as fighters, the multiple He 111s as bombers and reconnaissance aircraft and the Ju 52 as transports (all of which featured pre-World War Two technology). While in other countries, jets were flying, in Spain all the aircraft were obsolete, even before they had finished being built.

In 1953, the EdA had about 900 aircraft, although only 600 were in flightworthy condition, and even these were obsolete. For example, the main Spanish fighters at the end of 1953 were ten FIAT Cr.32s, eight BF 109s, two Polikarpov I-15s and 17 Polikarpov I-15bises. Fortunately, due to American interest in Western Europe, on 24 September 1953, a cooperation agreement between Spain and United States was signed known as the 'Pacto de Madrid' (the Madrid Pact).

This deal meant that modern aircraft, consisting mainly of jets, began to arrive in Spain under the Mutual Assistance Program (MAP). In exchange, Spain allowed the USAF to use several airbases at Rota, Morón, Torrejón, and more. The treaty also included: an agreement for mutual defence and financial assistance. But perhaps one of the most important parts of the deal was that CASA (a large Spanish aircraft manufacturer) would be in charge of doing the maintenance tasks for different USAF aircraft types.

A T-33A from Grupo 41 based at Zaragoza AB. This aircraft type soldiered on in the Grupo until it was replaced by the C-101 in 1981. The aircraft has an all-silver livery, as was usual in the T-33s, and the Ala 2 emblem (a tiger). Nowadays, this emblem is used by the Ala 15, with the motto 'Quien ose paga' ('Who dares pays').

In April 1954, the US began to supply modern aircraft to Spain. The first to arrive were Lockheed T-33A jets and some sea rescue Grumman HU-16As. The first six T-33s got to Spain in 1954, but soon 48 more had arrived thanks to the MAP. As this aircraft type was a training version of the famous F-80 Shooting Star, the T-33s were seen as a priority for the EdA to train pilots on how to fly jets (as the F-86F was the main aircraft that arrived through MAP).

The first T-33s (named the E.15 in the EdA) were deployed to the Escuela de Reactores at Talavera AB for training purposes. The 48 aircraft acquired by Spain arrived mainly from Chateauroux AB, American depots and some of them by ship. As the aircraft proved good for the role, 12 more T-33s (also ex-USAF aircraft) were acquired from US in 1964 (the last one arrived in Spain in November 1964). Most of the aircraft were T-33A-1s, although about 18 were T-33A-5s. The main difference between both aircraft was that the A-1 was armed with two Colt Browning M3 12.7mm machine guns, but the A-5 had no armament. During the 1960s, the A-1 lost its machine guns, and these were replaced by a TACAN navigation system.

The Escuela de Reactores was created on 10 December 1953 to house the T-33s that would arrive in March 1954. The first Spanish jet flew on 24 March 1954, marking a huge milestone for the EdA. From October 1958, F-86s arrived at the Escuela de Reactores to join with the T-33s. So, between 1958 and June 1969, the school's training course consisted of two parts: first flying the T-33s, then the F-86Fs. Last, the new pilots were deployed to the combat units (Alas/Wings). The T-33s were deployed to Escuadrón 731 (from 1965) and Escuadrón 732 (from 1971) at Talavera.

In addition, all the alas (1–6) received at least two T-33s for each squadron in order to provide each of the alas with jet trainers (about 25 F-86Fs were deployed across the different alas). At this time, the two-crewed F-86 did not exist, so the T-33 was a useful aircraft for this role.

From 1973 onward, all the T-33s left Talavera AB, as the new F-5s replaced the T-33s as advanced trainers, and joined Zaragoza AB. The aircraft were deployed to Ala 41 (Grupo 41) at Zaragoza. These T-33s were still intended for training at their new location, specifically refreshing jet pilots that were not in flying units. The last four surviving T-33s were used as tug targets during early 1985. Finally, in March 1985, after 31 years in service, the last T-33 was retired, ending the history of the first jet that ever flew within the EdA.

T-33A performance

Service Time with the EdA	1954–85
General Characteristics	
Wingspan	11.50m (37ft 9in)
Length	11.20m (36ft 9in)
Height	3.30m (9ft 11in)
Wing Area	21.80m² (69sq ft)
Weight	
Empty	3,775kg (8,322lb)
Max take-off	6,865kg (15,135lb)
Engine	1 x Allison J33-A-35

Others	
Maximum speed	985km/h (612mph)
Operative service ceiling	14,600m (47,900ft)
Combat range with fuel tanks	2,050km (1,274 miles)

Armament	
Inner	2 x Browning M2 12.7mm machine guns (350rpg)
Hardpoints	2 for up to 1,500kg (3,300lb)

Liveries

The T-33s were painted in all-metal finish. During the years of flying service within the EdA, the under-surfaces were coated in light blue, as can be seen in many pictures. The topside of the nose was coloured in black (differing depending on the aircraft's wing assignment), while the forward fuselage in front of the cockpit was painted in dark green to prevent flashes for the pilot. The typical markings on each aircraft were Spanish cockades, unit and aircraft numbers, and the St. Andrew's Cross.

The aircraft that were deployed to Talavera AB had the unit number (73) painted on both sides of the forward fuselage. However, from 1965, it changed to 731 (for Escuadrón 731) and from 1971 to 732 (for Escuadrón 732). When the alas received some T-33s, these aircraft used their new unit number, for example, 101 was used when an aircraft was from Ala 1, based at Manises. When at last the T-33 joined 41 Grupo, the aircraft changed their unit number to 41.

The Lockheed T-33A arrived in Talavera la Real in March 1954. This was the first jet in the Escuela de Reactores (Jet School). On 24 March 1954, the first Spanish jet took off from the Escuela de Reactores. The aircraft in the picture belonged to Escuadrón 732 based at Talavera la Real. Both are coated in all-metal finish, and the sole difference is the top fin is painted in grey on the aircraft in the foreground.

A T-33A from Escuadrón 101 based at Manises. The T-33As were used as trainers in all kinds of missions except for tactical or air defence, these being fulfilled by F-86s.

A rear-view of one of the T-33s deployed in Grupo 41. Notice the tiger badge at the rear fuselage with the text 'AMIGO' ('Friend'). This badge is still used by C-101s (Group 41) and F/A-18s (Ala 15) based at Zaragoza.

A beautiful side view of one of the Spanish T-33s, still without the St. Andrew's Cross painted on the tail.

Four T-33s, based at Zaragoza AB, show us their under surfaces and the inner sides of the wing tips; notice that the latter are painted in dark green, highlighting from the metal finish of the aircraft.

This is a superb frontal view of a T-33, where we can see the usual livery of this aircraft type: metal finish with under surfaces painted in light blue. Notice the Spanish markings: cockade, unit emblem, St. Andrew's Cross, unit number and aircraft number. (Public Domain by Dars Mol)

Several Spanish aircraft, lined up and painted in silver. In the foreground is a T-33 from Grupo 41, and behind you can see an F-86F and three F-5s. When the F-5s arrived at the EdA, the T-33s were replaced in their training role by these aircraft, which, unlike the T-33s, had been built in Spain.

Above: Two T-33s from Escuadrón 731 fly in formation in 1966. It was the first unit to receive this aircraft type. Thanks to the T-33s, many new Spanish pilots were trained to fly the modern jets that arrived in Spain from 1954.

Right: A T-33A at San Javier AB. The aircraft is yet to receive the typical Spanish markings, but it does have the aircraft type on the tail and the national marking in six different places.

Two T-33s are lined up at Zaragoza AB. Although most of the T-33s that arrived in Spain were T-33A-1s, some of them were T-33A-5s. After a training mission, both aircraft are again ready for the next one.

Chapter 2
North American F-86 Sabre

History

After the US-Spain agreements, the T-33s were the first jets that arrived in Spain, but the bulk of the deliveries were of another famous jet: the North American F-86F. This aircraft transformed Spanish aviation history and represented a huge milestone for the EdA.

On 30 June 1955, the first F-86F jet arrived at Getafe AB, marking a milestone in the history of Spanish aviation, and, in total, 270 Sabres were received during the five years until 1960, courtesy of the MAP. Getafe was the meeting point for the incoming F-86s; in the end, the speed with which the F-86s arrived meant that there were more than 100 F-86s outside the hangars at Getafe waiting for their ferry flight to their new unit. Between 1955–1957, the US supplied Spain with approximately 200 F-86F Sabres, 120 North American T-6D/G Texans, 30 Lockheed T-33As, five HU-16A Albatrosses, 15 Douglas C-47s, and several helicopters.

Almost all of the Spanish F-86s were ex-USAFE aircraft (from 36th FDW, 50th FBW, 86th FBW or 521st FDS and 514th FBS) coming from Germany, the Low Countries or Great Britain. However, the F-86F-40s were brand new and began to arrive in Spain in August 1956.

The last of the Spanish Sabres (C.5) was delivered to the EdA in July 1959, leaving Spain's total numbers as 18 F-86F-20s, 155 F-86F-25s, 32 F-86F-30s and 65 F-86F-40s. All the Sabres came from the USAFE, and although they were all different versions initially, all were updated in Spain (mostly by CASA) to F-86F-40-NA standard.

The first F-86Fs in Spain were deployed to Ala 1 (formed at Manises AB on 6 September 1955). The ala had two squadrons, Escuadrón 11 and Escuadrón 12, which had been formed with 25 aircraft each. Once the aircraft and pilots were ready, Escuadrón 11 began its service missions in October 1955 and Escuadrón 12 in April 1956. On 23 February 1956, when Ala 1 had 30 aircraft ready, American ambassador Henry Lodge officially 'delivered' the aircraft to Spain. The aircraft were manned by American pilots from their former bases in the US, Chateauroux AB or RAF Prestwick (both of the latter were bases were where the retired USAF aircraft were stored).

In the following years, other alas received the F-86s (25 aircraft to each escuadrón): Escuadrón 21 (from Ala 2, based at Valenzuela) in October 1957; Escuadrón 41 (which became Ala 4 from 1959, based at Son San Juan) in September 1956; Escuadrón 61 (based at Getafe) in 1958; and Escuadrón 51 in 1959 (from Ala 5, based at Morón). All the alas that had F-86s were under the command of the Mando de la Defensa Aérea (Air Defence Command). Escuadrón 98 was another unit where the Sabres were deployed (only 6 or 7 aircraft, based at Torrejón). Several 'Escuadrón de Alerta' ('Alert Squadrons') were created to watch over the Spanish airspace (usually armed with AIM-9B missiles). The Sabres from Escuadrón 41 were the first Spanish aircraft to be equipped with AIM-9B missiles.

The Spanish pilots improved their skills by flying the F-86s and, although intended for air defence, they practised strike missions too. Very soon, the Spanish pilots began combined air defence missions with USAFE aircraft (mainly with aircraft based at Valenzuela or Torrejón ABs). Thanks to the modern Sabres, Spain was also able to increase its relations with other air forces, starting exchange programmes

The North American F-86 arrived in the Escuela de Reactores in October 1958. Here, they were used to form Escuadrón de Aplicación y Tiro (Shot and Application Squadron), which provided flight and combat training for the new pilots. Then, 731 and 732 Escuadrones were formed. The aircraft shown in the pictures belonged to Escuadrón 732, based at Talavera la Real.

and joint exercises with the EdA. In 1957, Spain began to exchange whole squadrons with other countries as well, including Italy, Portugal and France.

During 1955–72, approximately 30 aircraft were lost in 75 accidents and 27 pilots killed, and from 1962, several F-86s were retired (and used as spare parts for F-86s that were still flying). Additionally, 29 F-86F-25s were returned to the USAF.

Roughly, 200 F-86Fs were in service in 1962 and, from 1964 until 1972 after the disbandment, the EdA went through a restructuring:

- Ala 1 became Ala 11 and held Escuadrón 112, which shortly after became Escuadrón 101.
- Ala 2 became Ala 12 and held Escuadrón 121.
- Ala 5 became Ala 15 and held Escuadrón 151.
- Ala 6 became the Ala 16 and held Escuadrón 161, which shortly after became Escuadrón 162, and a new unit, Escuadrón 161, that was set up to operate the F-104s.
- Escuadrón 98 became Escuadrón 981, which operated F-86Fs until 1967.

Everything was going very well for the EdA thanks to these modern jets, but, in 1957, the Sidi Ifni War for Spanish territories in Western Africa commenced. The situation in the Spanish African territories

When the Sabre arrived in Spain, it became the first jet fighter within the EdA and the backbone of the interceptor force, but it was necessary to instruct the new pilots on flying jets. The best fighter before the Sabre was the obsolete Bf 109F, so the capabilities of the EdA were increased greatly by their arrival.

The Spanish Sabres had an all-silver livery with Spanish cockades (in six positions) and St. Andrew's Cross in the tail. The colour of the band painted on the nose indicates the unit.

(Sahara and Sidi Ifni) was worsening so much that before the persistent attacks of Morocco at the end of 1957, Spain entered into an undeclared war to defend its possessions. Among the diverse types of aircraft that were sent into combat were HA-1112 M1Ls, Junkers Ju 52s, the CASA 2111 and the tandem trainers T-6 Texans. Frustratingly for the EdA, while Spain already had the F-86 Sabres in its possession, the conditions imposed by the United States stated that they could only be used on the Iberian Peninsula, thus forbidding the use of any US-gifted aircraft in the conflict. On 4 April 1965, four Sabres belonging to Ala 1 (Escuadrón 12) were deployed to Gando AB. This was the first deployment of Spanish jets to the Canary Islands, and although the aircraft only were at Gando for three days, it was an important display of Spanish strength to the country's western territories.

After the arrival of the F-104s in 1965, the F-86Fs and the F-104s became the backbone of the EdA. However, the ban on using American-gifted aircraft over Spanish African territories led to an important change in the new aircraft that Spain would acquire. New aircraft such as the Mirage III, F-5 and F-4C would arrive for the EdA over the following years, and the F-86's role was diminishing every day. During 1969–72, the F-86s were disappearing from combat and training units and being replaced by modern aircraft. The last air defence mission that a Spanish F-86 flew happened on 7 December 1972.

During and after 16 years of service, the F-86 remained an important feature in the EdA's history by being the force's first fighter jet. The Spanish F-86s racked up more than 360,000 flight hours, and thanks to the 270 F-86s that came and went, the expansion of the EdA and the creation of new units (alas and escuadrones) was made possible. This allowed the EdA to become more of an equal player against the other European air forces in terms of aircraft, tactics, and size.

During their service years, the Spanish F-86s accumulated more than 360,000 flight hours. For 17 years, the Sabre was the masterpiece of Spanish air defence. When the last Sabre was retired, in December 1972, they were replaced by a mix of aircraft, including the Mirage III, F-4, F-104 and F-5.

F-86F-40 Performance

Service Time in Spain	1955–72
General Characteristics	
Wingspan	11.40m (37ft 5in)
Length	11.90m (39ft)
Height	4.50m (14ft 9in)
Wing area	29.10m^2 (313sq ft)
Weight	
Empty	6,719kg (14,813lb)
Max take-off	9,375kg (20,668lb)
Engine	1 x General Electric J47-GE27
Others	
Maximum speed	1,091km/h (678mph) at sea level
Operative service ceiling	14,325m (46,998ft)
Combat range with fuel tanks	1,700km (1,065 miles)
Armament	
Inner	6 x Colt-Browning M-3 12.7mm machine guns (1,600 rounds)
Hardpoints	2 for AIM-9J Sidewinder AAM (wingtips) Several bombs and rockets (up to 670kg/1,477lb)

In this picture, we can see three of the first jet aircraft types that flew for the EdA. In the foreground is a F-86 from Escuadrón 102, a T-33A from Grupo 41 and a two-seat F-5 (SF-5B) from Ala 21.

Liveries

When the F-86s were deployed, they were coated in all-metal finish. In order to differentiate one unit from another, the nose tip was painted in a specific colour: Escuadrón 11 had red; Escuadrón 12 had blue; Escuadrón 21 had black; Escuadrón 41 had green; Escuadrón 51 had orange; Escuadrón 98 had green-yellow; and Escuadrón 61 had white. Though shortly after, the full painting of the tip was replaced by a simple band of colour across the nose.

In addition to the paintwork, the typical markings of cockades, unity and aircraft numbers or St. Andrew's Cross were added. Since 1959, Ala 1's aircraft have carried an emblem that was used by the Spanish 'Escuadrillas Azules' ('Blue Squadrons') within the Luftwaffe against the Soviets, consisting of a white circle with three birds in the middle (a hawk, a bustard and a blackbird). Of course, if an aircraft was transferred to another unit, its emblem would be used instead, for example, a cockerel for Ala 5 or a tiger for Ala 2, painted either on the rear fuselage (almost below the forward part of the fin), below the rear part of the cockpit or below the forward part of the cockpit (the position depended on the unit).

Above: A line up of F-86s from Escuadrón 111 await the upcoming mission. This aircraft represented an important step for the EdA, despite their weary-looking status when they arrived in Spain.

Right: Several F-86Fs line up at Son San Juan AB. These aircraft were based at Manises, as you can tell by the nose band (painted red for Escuadrón 101 and painted blue for Escuadrón 112) on the two aircraft in the foreground.

Above: Several Spanish Sabres flying low in May 1969 during a mission. The Sabres represented, for several years, the bulk of the EdA's force, with a total of 270 aircraft.

Left: Carlos Gómez, one of the courageous Spanish pilots that flew the Sabres. Thanks to this aircraft type and to their pilots, the EdA became a modern and powerful air force.

Below: A beautiful side view of a Spanish F-86. This jet type was the first modern fighter for the EdA.

Above: A F-86 from Escuadrón 112 at Son San Juan airport. The F-86s from Manises AB were the first Spanish fighter jets to fly to the Balearic Islands.

Right: A close-up of the nose and cockpit of an F-86, showing the typical all-silver livery with Spanish cockades. This picture was taken in 1968.

Below: Several pilots during a briefing before the next flight. In the background, we can see two F-86s.

Spanish Military Jets 1954–2022

Above: A F-86 at Tablada AB for maintenance duties at the Maestranza facilities. Note the grassy ground where the aircraft is being towed – this airstrip was not good enough for the jets.

Left: Two Sabres from Escuadrón 112 take off for their next patrol. Notice the big St. Andrew's cross on the tail and the all-metal finish.

Below: Coming back to Manises from Zaragoza in February 1968.

Chapter 3

HA-200 Saeta and HA-220 Súper Saeta

History

After the end of World War Two, the Spanish government tried to increase its air power with acquisitions of new aircraft, but most of the countries carried out a commercial blockade against it. Subsequently, Spanish authorities knew that the only way increase air power was by building aircraft in Spain itself. The main aircraft that Spain, through La Hispano Aviación S.A., managed to build during and after the war were the He 111, the Ju 52 and the Bf 109G (which was never built, but instead enabled development of the HA-1109 and HA-1112), which, as we have discussed, were already obsolete. Undeterred, however, the Spanish aircraft companies Hispano Aviación and CASA, helped by German engineers, went on to develop the best Spanish-manufactured aircraft at this time: the HA-200 Saeta (although the word is the same as for 'arrow', the word was chosen in reference to a typical Spanish song sung during the Holy Week in Seville, where the aircraft was built). It was the first Spanish-built jet, and it was designed by Willy Messerschmitt (the famous father of the Bf 109s and other important aircraft for Germany during World War Two).

Spanish-built Hispano Aviación HA-220 Súper Saetas, close to the Jerez AB. This aircraft was a single-seat improvement of the Saeta, and it was intended for close attack role. This aircraft entered into service in 1973 with Escuadrón 406 (Villanubla AB) and Escuadrón 214 (Morón AB) and had a two-tone camouflage (tan and dark green) with light blue under surfaces.

It was in 1951 that Willy Messerschmitt arrived in Spain to supervise the Spanish licensed manufacturing of the Bf 109. During this visit, the heads of Hispano Aviación talked with him about the development of a new two-crewed jet training aircraft in Spain, together with a small piston-engine training aircraft and a delta-winged jet fighter (these aircraft would eventually become the HA-200 Saeta, HA-100 Triana and HA-300, respectively). So, in 1952, a German-Spanish team led by Willy Messerschmitt started the work that concluded, three years later, with the HA-200. The chosen engine, the French Turbomeca Marboré II, were license-built in Spain by ENMASA.

The maiden flight of the Saeta was on 12 August 1955, taking off from San Pablo airport (Seville). The prototype was unarmed, but the second one (which made its first flight in 1957) was armed with two machine guns atop the nose. The Spanish government really liked the aircraft, and ten Saetas were ordered in 1957 and renamed HA-200R1. These aircraft were later armed with one cannon and sold to Egypt in 1960 as HA-200B, and 90 were license-built in Egypt as the Al-Qahira until 1969.

In 1959, the EdA ordered 30 HA-200A series aircraft (at the same time, the contract of Willy Messerschmitt ended, and he left the development of the Saeta). In June 1960, the first Saeta flew for the EdA; the aircraft started to be deployed to different units in the early 1960s as a trainer aircraft. It is known that at least ten HA-200As were tested at Talavera AB in 1963, and in 1964, 21 aircraft were deployed to Escuadrón 741 (based at Matacán) intended for basic training, although shortly after, these were redeployed to Escuadrón 431 from Ala 43, based at Villanubla AB. In EdA service, these aircraft were renamed C.10As, and their engines were Turbomeca Marboré IIs.

In 1963, the EdA ordered 55 Saetas; this time they were the improved HA-200Ds, with better engines and hydraulic and electric systems. These were to be deployed from late 1965 to Ala 43 based at Villanubla (at Valladolid, within Escuadrón 203) and to the Escuela Básica (Basic [training] School)

The first jet ever built in Spain was the HA-200 Saeta. This aircraft was designed by the well-known Willy Messerschmitt in 1955. This two-engine aircraft was built in the Triana quarter at Seville and demonstrated an absolutely superb performance. In total, 117 Saetas flew for the EdA: two prototypes, five pre-series, 30 HA-200As (E.14), 55 HA-200Ds (first E.14B then C.10) and 25 HA-220s Súper Saeta (C.10C).

The EdA HA-200 Saetas were named A.10 (attack version), C.10 (fighter version, which was also known as the A.10 after 1978) or E.14B (training). Since their arrival with the EdA, they were based at Villanubla, Matacán, San Javier, Gando and Morón de la Frontera (where the last HA-200 served in 204 Escuadrón until 1981 when they were retired). In this image, a Saeta is flying over the Canary Islands.

based at Matacán. These aircraft were renamed E.14B ('E' for 'training'). Forty of these aircraft were improved to HA-200E Súper Saeta standard and named C.10B. These aircraft had two Turbomeca Marboré VI engines, which boasted better performance than the Turbomeca Marboré II. Between 1968 and 1969, the 55 HA-200Ds were improved by adding two nacelles (Matra 38s) to increase their firepower. Thanks to this change, the aircraft also increased its fight capability in terms of power and velocity, and the name E.14B was replaced by C.10B in early 1968.

During 1971–72, an aerobatic team was created. Five Saetas took part in several Open Gates days at the airbases. After the team was disbanded, the aircraft were sent to Escuadrón 793 for the Academia General del Aire (AGA, Air General Academy).

In 1974, the aircraft deployed in Matacán were sent to Morón AB, where they flew until being withdrawn. The Saeta also resided in San Javier within Escuadrón 793 for the Academia General del Aire and from June 1972 as a basic trainer, and Gando AB, among other units. From Gando AB (attached to Escuadrón 462), these aircraft were used in combat missions during the ongoing conflicts in the Spanish West African territories. For example, in 1964, in the Spanish Sahara conflict, they were used not only as liaison and reconnaissance aircraft but as attack aircraft too, armed with rockets.

In 1976, Escuadrón 462 was disbanded and the C.10Bs were sent to Tablada AB with Escuadrón 793 and Escuadrilla 905. From 1980, all the Saetas and Súper Saetas were sent to Escuadrón 214 at Morón.

The aircraft was intended to have a jet trainer role, but due to the good performance of the basic Saeta, an attack variant was created. The EdA named the aircraft C.10 at the beginning, but this was changed to A.10 in 1978 in reference to its new attack role.

The HA-220 Súper Saeta (C.10C at the beginning but A.10C from 1978) was intended for a tactical and close support role and was entered into service in July 1973. Some of them were equipped with a photographic camera for reconnaissance missions, and its name changed to AR.10C. The main feature

A Súper Saeta photographed from a Saeta. Notice that the rear seat has been removed. It was replaced by a fuel tank that increased the aircraft's range. Notice that the unity number is not painted on the fuselage.

of the Súper Saeta was that this aircraft needed only one crew member, the second seat being replaced by a fuel tank. The first unit to receive the HA-220s was Escuadrón 406 based at Villanubla AB, and later all were redeployed to Escuadrón 214 at Morón AB.

From the end of the 1950s, the Saeta (a total of 97 HA-200As and Ds) and Súper Saeta (a total of 25 HA-220Es) soldiered on in the EdA until the early 1980s. Then, they were withdrawn after the arrival of their replacement in the training role: the C-101 Aviojet. The last unit to have Saetas was Escuadrón 214 at Morón, although this was before they were dispatched to Gando AB. The E.14A and A.10A/B were officially withdrawn on 15 November 1980, although the last one actually retired in 1981. During their 21 years in service, the Saetas achieved about 68,000 operational service flight hours and were the main training aircraft for hundreds of new pilots.

HA-200D Performance

Service Time in Spain	1960–81
General Characteristics	
Wingspan	10.932m (36ft)
Length	8.970m (29ft 5in)
Height	2.846m (9ft 4in)
Wing area	17.40m² (187sq ft)

Weight	
Max take-off	3,350kg (7,386lb)

Engine	2 x Turbomeca Marboré VI

Other	
Maximum speed	660km/h (410mph) at sea level
Operative service ceiling	13,000m (42,651ft)
Combat range with fuel tanks	1,400km (870 miles)

Armament	
Inner	2 x Breda CETME 7.7mm machine guns
Hardpoints	8 for bombs, rockets, cannon or fuel tanks

HA-220

Service Time in Spain	1973–81

General Characteristics	
Wingspan	10.932m (36ft)
Length	8.970m (29ft 5in)
Height	2.846m (9ft 4in)
Wing area	17.40m² (187sq ft)

Weight	
Max take-off	3,472kg (7,655lb)

Engine	2 x Turbomeca Marboré VI

Others	
Maximum speed	660km/h (410mph) at 6,000m
Operative service ceiling	13,000m (42,651ft)
Combat range with fuel tanks	1,700km (1,056 miles)

Armament	
Inner	2 x Breda CETME 7.7mm machine guns
Hardpoints	2 x 12.7mm machine guns (nacelles under the nose) 8 for bombs, rockets, cannon, fuel tanks (130 litre [34 US gal]), napalm bombs

Liveries

The HA-200 and HA-220 used different painting schemes during their service time depending on their role, although the under-surfaces in all types were always painted with light blue camouflage.

As the first role was training, it was considered necessary to have a high-visibility livery, which ultimately became the typical Saeta livery: anti-corrosion grey overall with red around the intakes and subsequently extending into a bolt outlined in white. The wingtips were painted red, although sometimes the tip received another colour.

With the arrival of new and improved attack Saetas, some aircraft were deployed to combat units, such as Escuadrón 462, and a new livery was needed. As the aircraft had to fly both over the Canary Islands and Spanish western territories, the paint scheme consisted of a tri-coloured camouflage (tan, brown and dark green). Usually, the upper half or two-thirds of the wing tip was painted in the camouflage scheme and the lower part in light blue or light grey. The HA-220s were built to be attack aircraft, so they began with a two-tone (tan and dark green) camouflage paint scheme. Although it was unusual in the Saeta, the Súper Saetas often bared the unit emblem at the top of the fin. Usually, the upper half of the wing tip was painted in the camouflage scheme and the lower part in light blue or light grey.

Two Ha 220 Súper Saetas from Morón AB are flying over southern Spain. Both the Saeta and the Súper Saeta represented big steps for the Spanish aeronautical industries. This achievement would continue with many other successful aircraft, such as the CASA C-212, C-101, CN-235, C-295 and collaborations in international projects such as the Eurofighter or the Airbus A400M.

A HA-220 Súper Saeta from Escuadrón 214 is seen flying over Sierra Nevada. This unit was the last in the EdA to operate these aircraft, having them until 1981. Notice the cross-shaped lines of the HA-220.

A HA-220 formation during a training flight. Notice the camouflage scheme and the small Spanish cockades and St. Andrew's Cross painted on the fin. As this aircraft was intended for combat missions, it was important to conceal as much of its shape as possible with this painting pattern.

Three HA-200Es (C.10B) are lined up at Villa Cisneros (Spanish West African territories) in 1974 in their classic training paint scheme. These aircraft were deployed to Escuadrón 462 based at Gando AB, although they were frequently sent to African territories.

A HA-220 from Escuadrón 214 lands at Jerez de la Frontera AB. Notice the name 'SAETA' painted on the nose. The good performance of the Saeta spurred on the manufacturing of the Súper Saeta.

The Saeta (this time a C.10B) was an enormous success for Spain. It was a milestone for the promising Spanish aircraft industries, which, some years after, would become very important and respected in Europe.

The HA-200R Saeta prototype at Paris Air Show at Le Bourget. It was in May 1957 when the Spanish jet was officially presented, and its first wholly foreign customer was Egypt. Notice the Hispano Aviación emblem (a flying stork) painted on the fin. (Ruth AS)

Two Saetas (C.10Bs) from Escuadrón 462 are parked at Villa Cisneros (in the Spanish Sahara, today renamed as Dajla) airport in 1975. This was the last year that Spain held its West African territories. Thanks to the excellent performance of the aircraft, the Saeta could land at rudimentary airstrips of sand or grass.

A tail view of a Saeta belonging to the AGA. Note the tri-tone camouflage typical of this type of aircraft.

A beautiful view of two Saetas flying over the cathedral of Seville, the city where these aircraft were manufactured.

This Saeta is a training aircraft for the students at San Javier. The C.10B was an aircraft that played an especially important training role within the EdA because it was manufactured with the EdA training necessities in mind.

Chapter 4

Lockheed F-104G Starfighter

History

After the arrival of the F-86s, the EdA had improved its ranking amongst the air forces of Europe. However, even these fighters were quickly looking older every day; they were not equipped with radar technology, and their firepower was insufficient when compared with the modern fighters of the 1960s. Taking this into account, in 1964, Spain asked for new and modern fighters from the US, specifically the Lockheed F-104G Starfighter. The reason why this aircraft was chosen by the EdA was that the F-104 was being acquired by many of the air forces of Western Europe (Germany, Italy, Belgium and the Low Countries), as well as Japan, Canada and the US. With this aircraft, the EdA hoped its rank would rise further still, as well as its capabilities and efficiency.

However, the US was initially reluctant to sell this aircraft type to Spain and offered 40 Convair F-102s from 431 and 497 squadrons (based at Zaragoza and Torrejón AB, respectively). The EdA refused the Convair, and the US offered used F-104Cs (from 157 Squadron, based at Morón de la Frontera); again, the Spanish answer was 'no'. The EdA wanted new aircraft to turn into the core of the force, so the negotiations continued. At last, Spain and the US reached an agreement, and in 1965 Spain received 18 Lockheed F-104G Starfighters (C.8) and three TF-104Gs (CE.8). The initial agreement was for 18 F-104Gs, two TF-104Gs and one F-104 flight simulator, but the last one was changed for another two seat TF-104 (the only one aircraft that belonged wholly to the EdA and was not part of the MAP agreement), and so an agreement was signed with Italy and Germany in order to use their flight simulator for the Spanish pilots' training. The F-104s were built by Canadair (Canada) and the TF-104s were built by Lockheed (US). The F-104G represented a considerable improvement in Spanish air power. A pilot compared the F-86 and F-104 performance, saying that the first was like a car and the second was like a race car. At last, Spain had its first supersonic aircraft.

Once the aircraft arrived in Spain, the EdA HQ had to decide where to deploy the new aircraft. There was some debate between which of two bases was better suited to the F-104G: Morón de la Frontera or Torrejón de Ardoz; the winner was the latter. At that time in 1965, Torrejón AB was home to the Ala 6 (with North American F-86Fs), so it was decided to select most of the airmen and ground crew for the F-104 unit from this ala. Additionally, four pilots (two lieutenants and two NCOs) were chosen from each of the alas across the EdA to join to the newly formed F-104 unit. Several requirements were necessary to enter the unit; for example, only aviators with more than 500 F-86 Sabre flight hours could be accepted.

In November 1964, four Spanish pilots arrived in the US for the training course. First, they were sent to the USAF Language School (Lackland, Texas), then to Randolph AFB and finally to Luke AFB (Phoenix, Arizona), where the F-104 Combat Pilot School was based. During the course, the Spanish airmen received many theoretical classes and had 40 flight hours. The other pilots and ground crew were trained in Spain at Torrejón AB thanks to a Mobile Training Unit with the main aircraft that had been acquired from the US.

Four F-104Gs fly over the Entrepeñas and Buendía swamps. The two F-104Gs closest have the unit number (UN) from 161 Escuadrón painted in the forward fuselage, but the other two aircraft lack it. It is noteworthy the flaps are in take-off position, because the aircraft needed to be as slow as the T-33 when the picture was taken in April 1965.

Further training of the pilots that remained in Spain was undertaken by two American instructors (two captains from the USAF) and the four Spanish pilots that were trained in the US. In the last months of 1965, Spanish pilots went first to Italy (Grazzanise AB, Napoli) then to Germany from March 1966 (Jever AB in northern Germany) for training in the flight simulator.

The F-104s arrived in Spain in three batches; all were shipped by American light aircraft carriers and delivered to Rota NAS.

- First batch: 15 January 1965. Five F-104Gs and two TF-104Gs. They flew to Torrejón AB on 4–17 February.
- Second Batch: 12 June 1965. Thirteen F-104Gs. They flew to Torrejón AB on 16–25 June.
- Third batch: 5 January 1966. One TF-104. It flew to Torrejón AB on 26 January.

The F-104 unit, although always being deployed at Torrejón AB, changed its name several times. When the aircraft arrived for the first time, the F-104s were deployed to Escuadrón 61 (from Ala 6). Escuadron 61 only lasted from February to April 1965. At that time, the name was changed to Escuadrón 161 (belonging to Ala 6, now Ala 16, because, in early April 1965, 6 turned into 16 after a restructuring of the EdA). Escuadrón 161 lasted from April 1965 to November 1967. In 1967, another

Although the F-104 was involved in many accidents in the other air forces with which it flew, in Spain no F-104G was ever lost. Indeed, during their operational service, the Spanish F-104Gs achieved 17,059 flight hours between 1965 and 1972 without losses. This aircraft is a TF-104G, which at the end of its life with the EdA was delivered to the Turkish Air Force.

EdA restructuring meant that the F-104 unit modified its name again, turning into Escuadrón 104 (this time the unit belonged to no ala, as it was independent). Escuadrón 104 lasted from November 1967 to May 1972. In May 1972, the unit was no longer independent as it was framed into Ala 12; it kept its name (Escuadrón 104), but only for a few days (27–31 May). The last name change was in early April 1972, when the unit became Escuadrón 122 (still belonging to Ala 12; 121 Escuadrón received the F-4Cs).

The official presentation of the Escuadrón 61 took place on 5 March 1965. On 8 March 1965, the Spanish F-104 flights started, and on 9 April, the official presentation for the press and public took place. It was during the Desfile de la Victoria (Victory Parade) where four F-104s flew over Madrid. Although, it was not until July 1965 that the last pilots arrived and the Escuadrón roster was complete.

On 24 September 1965, Escuadrón 161 joined the Air Defense Command, taking part in the *Red Eye* exercise. In 1967, it began the AIM-9B Sidewinder AAM real fire training. During June 1968, the first flight out of Spain with these aircraft occurred, when they flew to Italy for an exercise. This was a real step forward for the EdA in terms of it improving its relationship with other European air forces, from which it learned new technologies and ways of working. After Italy, the Spanish F-104s paid a visit to Germany.

A lonely F-104G takes off from Torrejón AB showing the light grey livery, only disrupted by the white wings. At this time, it belonged to Escuadrón 161, although, from 29 November 1967, Escuadrón 161 became Escuadrón 104.

The operational life of the F-104 in Spain lasted only seven years. Maintenance of the F-104 was not easy, as the escuadrón lacked the spare parts necessary to make sure all of its F-104s were flight ready. Therefore, it was not unusual that an aircraft could be out of work because of the lack of spare parts, and in extreme circumstances this led to the cannibalization of other F-104s. On 21 May 1972, the Spanish F-104s flew together for the last time during the Desfile de la Victoria, and only ten days later, Escuadrón 122 was converted to the new F-4Cs and the F-104Gs began to be withdrawn from use.

On 1 June 1972, the F-104s were symbolically returned to the US, although they kept flying until 25 January 1973 (when the last F-104 took off from Torrejón AB) to deliver them in flightworthy condition to the USAF. However, before being fully returned to the US, some Spanish F-104s were gifted to Greece and Turkey in 1972 by Spain. Ten (nine F-104Gs and one TF-104G) were delivered to the Polemikí Aeroporía (Greek Air Force) and 11 (ten F-104Gs and two TF-104Gs) to the Hava Kuvvetleri (Turkish Air Force).

During their seven years of service, no F-104s were lost while flying with the EdA, unlike the other air forces for which the F-104 flew. The total F-104 flight hours were 1,705,915. In February 1966, and thanks to this successful career for the EdA, Lockheed granted the Spanish F-104 unit the Flight Safety Award, having achieved over 8,000 flight hours without losses.

The F-104 was not just important for Spain as a fighter but also as a push for the Spanish aeronautical industry, as from 1965, CASA was entrusted with the maintenance programme for the F-104s based in Spain. Additionally, the need for the Spanish F-104 pilots to complete the training in Italy and Germany helped to build relationships with other air force units and personnel, which would prove very important when Spain joined NATO several years after.

F-104G Performance

Service Time in Spain	1965–72
General Characteristics	
Wingspan	6.68m (22ft)
Length	16.69m (54ft 9in)
Height	4.11m (13ft 5in)
Wing area	18.22m²
Weight	
Empty	6,387kg (14,081lb)
Max take-off	13,054kg (28,779lb)
Wing loading	723kg/m²
Engine	J79-GE-11A

A F-104G (C.8-10) landing at Torrejón AB. The F-104G was the only supersonic interceptor aircraft in the EdA for five years. This aircraft arrived in Spain on 6 June 1965 (American code FG-642) and was coded in Spain as 161-20 in 1965. It was then reserialled as 104-20 in 1967 and 104-10 in 1968. On 28 January 1974, it crashed near Polati when flying with Turkish markings.

Other	
Maximum speed	2,125km/h (1,320mph)
Cruise speed	Mach 0.95
Operative service ceiling	17,680m (58,005ft)
Combat range with fuel tanks	1,200km (746 miles)

Armament	
Inner	Vulcan M-61 20mm cannon (4,000rpm)
Hardpoints	4 for AIM-9B Sidewinder AAM Provision for bombs and rockets (up to 1,800kg/3,968lb)

Liveries

The F-104s and TF-104s delivered to Spain had a similar camouflage scheme. The fuselage was all in anti-corrosion semi-matte light grey finish, except the fuselage's tail, which was metallic. The upper wings were painted in white, and the radome in medium grey. The upper part of the nose (in front of the cockpit) was painted in dark green to avoid the sun blinding the pilot. Almost every F-104G and the TF-104G had the same scheme. One exception was the last TF-104G that arrived in Spain, coded CE.8-3, which was painted in an all-metal finish. The letters and numbers were painted in black, and of course the national roundels were in six positions with the St. Andrew's Cross on the tail.

This beautiful picture of CE-8.23 shows the overall metal finish scheme that was used by the Spanish F-104s, with the upper part of the nose painted in black. In addition, you can notice the escuadrón emblem consisting of a cat's head with the motto 'No le busques tres pies' (literally 'Do not look for three feet' but meant more along the lines of 'Do not split hairs').

In the foreground, you can see the TF-104G CE.8-3 104-23 parked at Torrejón AB. This was the only F-104 that fully belonged to the EdA. The TF-104s played an important role in the training of the new pilots for the escuadrón. Note the angled wings typical of this aircraft and the Spanish cockades on the wing and fuselage.

A wonderful picture of the F-104G displayed at the Museo del Aire de Cuatro Vientos (now known as the Museo de Aeronáutica y Astronáutica). In homage to its origin as a German aircraft, the starboard half of the aircraft is painted as C.8-15 (104-15) from Ala 12, while the aircraft port half is painted in Luftwaffe scheme and markings (26-23). (Public domain by Garrapata)

Another view of the F-104G displayed at the Museo del Aire de Cuatro Vientos. This aircraft was actually a F-104G from Jagdbombergeschwader 36 from the Luftwaffe. The real C.8-15 was delivered to the Turkish Air Force and recoded 4-733. (Public domain by Contando Estrelas from Vigo, España/Spain)

This Greek F-104G is displayed on concrete blocks in a park at Athens. This aircraft was one of the ones delivered from Spain in 1972. The aircraft (C.8-3 for the EdA) was coded 161-13 in 1965 for Escuadrón 161, 104-13 in 1967 for Escuadrón 104 and 104-03 for 104 Escuadrón in 1968 while flying for the EdA, then FG-717 when it was delivered to the Greek Air Force. (Jerry Gunner, Attribution 2.0 Generic CC BY 2.0, www.flickr.com/people/13722921@N06)

This TF-104G was a newcomer to Spain when this image was taken in 1965. Notice that, although the aircraft is bearing the Spanish cockades and the St. Andrew's Cross, it still is coded TG-279 (USAF) from before it was renamed 161-02 (with Escuadrón 161). When this aircraft was withdrawn from the EdA, it was was delivered to the Turkish Air Force and coded 9-279. (Public domain by René Francillon)

A close-up of the UN and emblem of the F-104G displayed at the Museo del Aire de Cuatro Vientos. Escuadrón 104 operated from November 1967 to May 1972. (Public domain by Contando Estrelas from Vigo, España/Spain)

Chapter 5
Dassault Mirage III

History

In the late 1960s, Spain once again needed new and modern jets to add to the F-86s and a handful of F-104s. The Ifni War (1957–58) experience showed that the political limitation in the use of American-made aircraft made the defence of territories very difficult. Therefore, alongside the building of wholly Spanish-made aircraft, it was also necessary to acquire new aircraft from sources with no restrictions. Several aircraft were selected as candidates: the Dassault Mirage III, McDonnell Douglas F-4C Phantom, SAAB J-35 Draken and SEPECAT Jaguar. At that time, France was the main European aircraft manufacturer, so Spain entered into negotiations to buy its chosen modern jet: the Mirage III.

The negotiations started in 1969, and the agreement was sealed in 1970 – on 27 February 1970, 30 aircraft were ordered from Marcel Dassault. At the beginning, the Spanish government had

A Mirage III from Escuadrón 111 flying near Manises AB, where this aircraft type was based. From May 1971, they were deployed to the Ala 11, which comprised Escuadrón 111 and Escuadrón 112. Note the typical green and grey Mirage III livery and the big St. Andrew's Cross.

Some Mirage III EEs (C.11) during a flight over Spain. These French aircraft represented a change in the Spanish combat aircraft source, which until that date had been the US only. On 30 June 1992, the Mirage III was retired from the EdA.

the intention to license-build the Mirage III in Spain, but the aircraft was needed as soon as possible, so the solution was the purchase of some Mirage III EEs and III DEs. With the purchase of the Mirage IIIs, Spain was sending a message to the US, making it clear that Spain no longer depended on just American help. In February–March 1970, eight Spanish pilots and 30 crewmen were sent to Dijon-Longvic AB (France) for training in the new aircraft with the Escadre de Chasse 2/2 'Côte d'Or'.

While the idea at the beginning was to buy 30 EEs and six Des, in 1970, Spain acquired 24 Mirage III EE (C.11) single-seat fighters and six Mirage III DE (CE.11) two-seaters. In EE and DE, the second E was for España (Spain). Notice that the Mirage III DE had neither radar nor Doppler. Therefore, they were not as suitable for combat as the EEs, although it did have cannons and could include AIM-9 missiles. The delivery of the first three of eight Mirage IIIs to the EdA took place at Dijon-Longvic AB on 10 April 1970. The eight total Mirage IIIs (first intended for French units but then selected for Spain) arrived at Manises AB (Spain), four coming from Dijon and four later from Luxeuil on 13 June 1970.

The Mirage III EE was one of the most advanced aircraft of its time, with a fully integrated weapons system, a Thomson CSF Cyrano IIB multifunction radar, a Marconi Elliot Doppler radar and armament intended for short (Sidewinder) and medium range (MATRA R.530). This was the first aircraft type within the EdA that had medium-range missile capabilities.

These French-designed aircraft were deployed to the Ala de Caza 10 (Fighter Wing) (formed of Escuadrón 101 and Escuadrón 103) based at Manises, specifically to Escuadrón 101. By the late 1970s, Spain had 12 Mirage IIIs in service (between 1970 and October 1972, all 30 purchased aircraft were delivered). But, on 16 December 1970, a two-seater Mirage III DE crashed (both crewmen survived), so the government decided to acquire a new two-seater version, which was delivered on 25 July 1973. Therefore, the total number of Mirage IIIs acquired by Spain was 31 (24 EEs and seven DEs).

Shortly after, on 3 June 1971, Ala 10 was renamed Ala 11 and constituted Escuadrón 111. Then, Escuadrón 112 was added on 12 January 1972. The radio codename was 'Dólar' for the 111 and 'Rublo' for the 112.

The Mirage IIIs became the backbone of the fighter branch within the EdA, and they were intended for the 'permanent alarm service', established on 26 March 1973, that allowed the two Mirage III EEs to be fully armed (two cannons and two AIM-9s) and ready to scramble 365 days a year, 24 hours a day. The Mirage III fulfilled this role until 14 March 1989.

Fortunately, these aircraft never saw combat, but that did not mean that they avoided having to take part in real combat missions. For example, when the political status with Morocco was worsening during 1975, four Mirage IIIs (Two from Escuadrón 111 and two from 112) were deployed to Gando AB (and secondarily to El Aaiún AB in the Spanish Sahara). Shortly after, in autumn 1975, when the risk of war in the Sahara was increasing, 12 Mirage IIIs (and 12 pilots) were on alert status, ready to be sent to the Canary Islands when necessary.

From 1982, the Mirage III was qualified to use the improved AIM 9P-3 Sidewinder (some modifications had to be made as the aircraft could only launch French-made missiles initially). Still, the 'Plancheta' ('iron', as the aircraft was dubbed by the pilots because of its shape) had a handful of years of service within the EdA.

One of the seven Mirage III DE (CE.11) two-seaters that Spain purchased. This aircraft, which is flying close to Manises AB, has a little St. Andrew's Cross painted on the tail but has no Ala 11 badge. When the most modern F-1 arrived in Spain, this powerful fighter was replaced.

By 1993, it was evident that the aircraft was getting old and required an overhaul. The plan was to improve the avionics, accessories, equipment and instruments. In addition, it was planned to add an inflight refuelling probe and canards (an important change as this could decrease the take-off and landing runs). With these changes, the life of the aircraft would be extended by 2,500 flight hours. Thanks to the new avionics, the aircraft could be armed with modern AIM-9 Sidewinder, AGM-65G Maverick and AGM-88 HARM and pods for electronic warfare. Within the EdA, the new aircraft would be renamed C.11M ('M' for modernised). The plan was for the works to be done at CASA's facilities, but none of these plans ever came to fruition, and the plan was cancelled on 6 August 1991. The main reason for this was that the Spanish government did not have the necessary funding to complete the overhaul, and it was considered to be a financially better move to focus on improving the most modern Spanish Mirage F-1s, rather than the older Mirage IIIs.

On 1 October 1992, the last flight of the Mirage IIIs took place over Manises AB, the last service flight having been on 30 September. During the farewell display, eight Mirage IIIs shared the limelight with six newcomer Mirage F-1s. Still, 16 EEs and five DEs were flyable, but their time had ended. The last 14 Mirage IIIs that landed at Manises AB did their last ferry flight to Getafe to be scrapped on 14–23 October 1992.

For most of their service lives, the Mirage IIIs were ready for action. Only during the last years, when it was known that the aircraft would be retired, did Ala 11 have a shortage of spare parts for the Mirages.

The Mirage flew for the EdA for over 22 years, and ten aircraft were lost in accidents and two pilots died. Although at the beginning, the Mirage IIIs were intended mainly for air-to-air missions (about 70 per cent) and strike missions (about 30 per cent), during their last year of service the Mirage IIIs increased their strike role (to about 75 per cent). These wonderful aircraft achieved 8,051,225 operational service flight hours (during 75,172 sorties), becoming one of the best Spanish air defence aircraft.

The high velocity needed for take-off and landing was typical of the Mirage IIIs. In order to slow down the velocity and shorten the landing, the Mirage IIIs had braking parachutes fitted in the tail. Additionally, a trapping net was installed at Manises AB to stop any aircraft flying too fast when landing.

Mirage III EE Performance

Service Time in Spain	13 June 1970–30 September 1992
General Characteristics	
Wingspan	8.22m (27ft)
Length	14.15m (46ft 5in) (EE), 15.03m (49ft 3in) (DE)
Height	4.25m (14ft)
Wing area	34.85m^2 (375sq ft)
Weight	
Empty	7,050kg (15,543lb)
Max take-off	13,500kg (29,763lb)
Engine	1 x SNECMA Atar 9C
Other	
Maximum speed	2,716km/h (1,688mph) at 12,000m
Operative service ceiling	17,000m (55,774ft) at Mach 1.8
Combat range with fuel tanks	2,300km (1,429 miles)
Armament	
Inner	2 x DEFA 552 30mm cannon (125rpg)
Hardpoints	5 for: 2 x AIM-9 Sidewinder AAM 1 x MATRA R.530 missile (under the fuselage) Several kinds of bombs and rockets (up to 4865kg)

Liveries

Due to the speed with which the aircraft were purchased, the Spanish Mirage III's livery was the same as in the Armée de l'Air (French Air Force). This scheme was introduced to French Mirage III Es in January 1968 and consisted of dark grey-blue and dark grey-green for the upper surfaces and matt aluminium for the under surfaces. During all the years that the Mirage IIIs flew for the EdA, they wore the same scheme.

Besides the typical markings (cockades, unit and aircraft numbers and St. Andrew's Cross), these aircraft had Ala 11's badge painted on the engine air intakes: a white circle with three birds in the middle (a hawk, a bustard and a blackbird) and the sentence 'Vista, suerte y al toro', which means 'Sight, luck and towards the bull'. This sentence was traditionally used by bullfighters when entering the bullfighting ring.

For the unit number, in the beginning, the number 101 was used (and 103, but only because of a French mistake that led to 103 being incorrectly painted on three to four aircraft before arriving in Spain), then 111 and 112 (from 1971–72) and finally 11, having joined Ala 11 in 1986.

A Mirage III parked at Manises AB. This aircraft could be fitted with AIM-9 or Matra Magic missiles. Note the external fuel tank under the port wing and the weapons on the floor.

An interesting rear view of a Mirage III DE landing with the braking parachute open. The high speed required for the landing was one of the downfalls of this superb aircraft.

This Mirage III EE (112-3) is taking off from Manises AB. Notice the two external fuel tanks under the wings, which carried up to 1,700 litres each.

111-14 takes off from Manises AB. Notice two features of the two-seater Mirage III: the radome is painted in the same way as the rest of the aircraft, except the black top (the Mirage III EE had it painted all in black) and the white curtain in the back seat intended for blind flight training.

One of the Mirage III EEs (C.11-1) selected for the 'permanent alarm service' resting under its shelter. There were two aircraft on this alert service; the first had to be ready in five minutes and the second one in 30 minutes.

Two proud pilots of a Mirage III: 'el Buzo' (the Diver) and 'el Bubi'. When this aircraft arrived in Spain, it represented an important step for the EdA, and new and modern technology had to be learned by pilots and ground crew. Notice Ala 11's emblem painted on the air intake.

A Mirage III EE from Escuadrón 112 during one of its flights over Spain. Note the smooth profile of this aircraft when flying, which enabled high speeds up to 2,716km/h.

An interesting picture of a Mirage III EE fitted with the medium-range MATRA R.530 missile in the centre pylon. The bulge under the forward cockpit was for the Doppler radar.

Pilots were much more important than the aircraft. Here, several Mirage III pilots from Escuadrón 112 smile for the camera in front of a line-up of their mounts. Notice the launching pod for the AIM-9 missile under the starboard wing in the closest aircraft.

A beautiful view of the Mirage III. It looks majestic and powerful, armed with MATRA R.530 missile in the centre pylon. Notice the typical Spanish markings under the wings and fuselage.

A formation of four Mirage IIIs from Escuadrón 112 during a mission. This aircraft meant a change in the Spanish purchasing of aircraft, which, until that moment, had been focused solely in the US.

A Mirage III from Escuadrón 112 flying over the Mediterranean coast of Spain, near their airbase at Manises.

The first delivery of a Mirage III to the EdA took place at Dijon-Longvic AB on 10 April 1970. Several Spanish pilots stand in front of a French Mirage III at Dijon on 23 May 1970.

The special stratospheric suit for the Mirage III pilots. While provided, this suit was not used, as these types of flights were not useful.

Chapter 6
Northrop F-5

History

In the 1960s, the Spanish government formed an agreement with Northrop to license-build the F-5 Freedom Fighter. CASA was the aircraft manufacturer selected to build 70 F-5s: 36 single-seaters called SF-5A (C.9) and 34 two-seaters called SF-5B (CE.9). Therefore, by 1968, CASA facilities in Getafe became the nest of one of the most important jets flying for the EdA.

The building of the aircraft began with eight two-seater SF-5Bs, which were sent to Spain from Northrop as kits in different stages of assemblage. The training of pilots for the new aircraft was a priority, so in 1968, six pilots and 12 crewmen from the EdA were sent to Williams AFB (Arizona) to learn all about the F-5s, in order to teach new pilots and crewmen in Spain.

The first Spanish F-5 took its maiden flight in May 1968. At that time, 18 of the SF-5As were modified as a reconnaissance aircraft named SRF-5A (CR.9). The first SF-5-equipped unit was the Escuadrón 202 (based at Morón), with the first arriving on 7 January 1970. The first aircraft that arrived were nine SF-5Bs, designed to begin the training of the new SF-5A pilots. Both Escuadrón 202 and Escuadrón 204 were supplied with the new SF-5A and SF-5Bs. On 12 November 1970, Talavera AB gained its first three SF-5Bs. This unit subsequently used these aircraft as advanced jet trainers.

One of the 18 SF-5As that were modified to be a reconnaissance aircraft with attack role capabilities, known within the EdA as an AR.9. Up to four cameras can be placed into the aircraft's nose in six different configurations. Note the nose when compared with the fighter version. When the aircraft was delivered to EdA, it had a silver livery, which was replaced by the tri-coloured one after several years. Close to the AR.9 is an Orion.

One year later, in 1971, Escuadrón 202 was deployed to the Escuela de Reactores and renamed Escuadrón 731. The same thing happened to the second SF-5 unit equipped, Escuadrón 204, which was turned into Escuadrón 732 attached to the Escuela de Reactores. Therefore, it was in 1971 that the F-5s started their role as trainers.

As new modern fighters arrived in Spain, the F-5 changed its role to attack aircraft and with this came a name change: C.9 became A.9, CE.9 became AE.9, and CR.9 became AR.9.

Meanwhile, on 15 April 1971, Ala 21 was created in Morón and consisted of Escuadrón 211 'Gallo' and Escuadrón 212 'Sisón', which replaced the Escuadrón 202 and Escuadrón 204 after their relocation. At the end of 1971, the last Spanish SF-5 was delivered to EdA. Escuadrón 211 was an attack squadron (equipped with SF-5As and SRF-5As), and 212 was a reconnaissance squadron (equipped with SRF-5As and SF-5Bs). In Ala 21, the SF-5s flew together with the HA-220 Súper Saeta. For 21 years, from Morón AB, the F-5s fulfilled mainly many fighter bomber attack, close air support and reconnaissance missions with a secondary air defence role.

In 1975, the first F-5s were deployed to Gando AB (Canary Islands) from Morón, where they stayed until 1982. The reason was the conflict between Spain and Morocco after Spain left the Spanish Sahara in 1975. The existing Texans and Saetas had to be replaced by a modern fighter, and the F-5 was chosen. On 4 February 1976, Escuadrón 212 was disbanded. Subsequently, half of the aircraft remained with Escuadrón 211 (Morón), and half were sent to Escuadrón 464 at Ala 46 (based at Gando). The F-5 was 'chosen' to be deployed to Gando because the more-powerful Mirage IIIEE/DEs, F-1CEs and F-4Cs had to watch over continental Spain. From Gando, the F-5s (SF-5A, SF-5B and SRF-5A) took part in many missions between Africa and the Canary Islands, defending the Spanish interests.

As new modern fighters arrived in Spain, the F-5 changed its role to attack aircraft and the name C.9 became A.9. The aircraft in the picture is painted with a beautiful tri-coloured livery suitable for that role.

Some F-5s lined up, showing us the different camouflage schemes and St. Andrew's Cross size they had.

They were usually armed with both cannons and three drop tanks. Although the war did not begin, more than 500 war missions were fulfilled by these fighters in the area. Six years after the F-5 arrived in the Canary Islands, they were replaced by the F-1s from Escuadrón 462.

In 1987, the Escuela de Reactores based at Talavera became Ala 23, specifically intended for strike and fighter training. Consequently, Escuadrón 731 became Escuadrón 231 and the Escuadrón 732 became Escuadrón 232. In November 1992, the F-5As and F-5RFs from Ala 21 were deployed to Ala 23, taking over from other historical jet trainers, the T-33 and the venerable F-86, at Talavera la Real AB.

In 1989, after an F-5 accident where a wing broke and two pilots died, the EdA decided to ground all of its F-5s until it had detected the cause. During this time, many F-5s were retired. For the aircraft that were not retired, but were still getting older, it was necessary to perform an overhaul in order to elongate their service lives. The first overhauling took place between 1991 to 1995 in CASA facilities at Getafe, and 22 two-seat aircraft had their avionics, engines and landing gear improved, becoming similar to newbuilt aircraft.

From 2001 to 2007, the aircraft were improved again, enabling them to fly into the 2020s, and their name was changed to F-5M ('M' for modernised) or F-5BM. Some main improvements included better avionics, VOR/ILS and Tacan navigation systems, V/UHF communication systems, a new cockpit with new virtual radar for training, HOTAS and modern digitisation. The first of the upgraded aircraft were delivered in 2003. The 22 upgraded F-5s, named SF-5M, still fly for the EdA as advanced combat trainers deployed to the Ala 23 (Escuadrón 231 'Patas negras' [Black legs] and Escuadrón 232). Additionally, F-5Ms are sometimes used as target tug aircraft (A/A37U-15).

Thanks to their improved performance, the F-5M is a suitable aircraft for the training of future F-18 and Eurofighter (4th and 5th generation aircraft) pilots. Nowadays, 19 F-5Ms still operate from Talavera AB. It is estimated that the F-5Ms will be replaced by a modern trainer from 2028 onwards.

The F-5As, F-5RF and F-5Ms have been, and still are, the training jets with the highest availability/cost ratio ever to fly for the EdA. After 51 service years, the F-5s achieved more than 170,000 operational service flight hours and had been flown by more than 1,000 new jet pilots as an advanced jet trainer. However, mainly due to its training role, some aircraft have been lost during accidents, and 24 pilots lost their lives while flying for Ala 21, Ala 23, Ala 46 and CLAEX.

F-5A Performance

Service Time in Spain	1970–Current
General Characteristics	
Wingspan	7.70m (25ft 3in)
Length	14.38m (47ft 2in)
Height	4.01m (13ft 2in)
Wing area	15.79m² (170sq ft)
Weight	
Empty	3,667kg (8,084lb)
Max take-off	9,374kg (20,666lb)
Engine	2 x General Electric J85-GE-13
Other	
Maximum speed	1,487km/h (924mph) at 11,000m
Operative service ceiling	15,390m (50,492ft)
Combat range with fuel tanks	2,600km (1,616 miles)
Armament	
Inner	2 x M-39 20mm cannons (280rpg)
Hardpoints	2 for AIM-9J Sidewinder AAM (wingtips)
	5 for bombs and rockets (up to 2,000kg/4,409lb)

Liveries

The F-5 is one of the EdA's aircraft that had been painted in many different schemes; the fact it has been flying for the EdA for more than 50 years may explain it. At the beginning, when the first F-5s arrived at the combat and training units, they had an all-metal or silver finish (metallised grey), with the upper part of the nose (in front of the cockpit) painted in dark green to avoid the sun blinding the pilot.

Then, when new and modern jets arrived in Spain, the F-5 changed to an attack role and the all-metal finished livery was replaced by a beautiful tri-coloured one (sand, brown and dark green) called the 'lizard scheme'. The under surfaces were painted light grey.

Nowadays, and since early 1994, the F-5s from Ala 23 are painted in a new scheme; this time is a standard light grey livery that replaced the metal and lizard schemes. The tip is coated in dark grey.

The letters and numbers were painted in black, and of course the national roundels were in six positions with the St. Andrew's Cross on the tail. During the early years, the large unit number was painted under the cockpit, but nowadays they are a more normal size. The St. Andrew's Cross on the rudder was eventually repainted in low-visibility markings. The unit's emblems are painted on the fin.

Two F-5s flying as fighters, which we know because of the aircraft number painted on the tail, 'C' after caza or fighter. They have a silver livery, as was usual during the '70s.

Seventy F-5s were license-built in Spain between 1968 and 1971, and in 1971, these were all in service. After many improvements and changing of roles, this superb aircraft is still used as an advanced combat trainer for Spanish pilots. In this picture, we see one of the 22 upgraded F-5s, named SF-5M (AE.9 in Spain), still deployed in the Ala 23.

A beautiful picture of the one of the remaining F-5s flying for the EdA. These F-5Ms (AE.9) might be replaced in the coming years in the advanced trainer role by the Airbus Future Jet Trainer.

Above: Sometimes the F-5 acts as a target tug. This AR.9 from Escuadrón 212 is parked close to the A/A37U-15 target at Gando AB. Note the cock emblem typical of Morón AB units.

Left: A close-up of an A.9 from Ala 21 based at Morón. Notice both 20mm M-39 cannons in the aircraft nose. This cannon, although designed in late '40s, was used in different aircraft from the early 1950s through to the 1980s.

Several A.9s from Ala 23 are lined up while in the background two F/A-18 are manoeuvring. It is noteworthy that at the time this picture was taken, the light grey livery was not in use yet.

Above: A beautiful shot of one of the 19 F-5Ms still in service at Talavera AB. Notice the smooth lines of the aircraft and the low-visibility Ala 23 emblem painted on the fin (a bird head, a frontal view of the F-5 and five stars).

Right: Another view of an AE.9 from Ala 23. This time the picture is older, so the aircraft is painted in all-metal finish. Comparing with the picture before, note the colourful emblem and the large size of the St. Andrew's Cross and Spanish cockades.

A CE.9 from Escuadrón 212, based at Morón AB, flies near the Rock of Gibraltar (Peñón de Gibraltar). From time to time, the Spanish jets showed their cockades in that area.

Three F-5s from Escuadrón 464 coming in to land. It was necessary that modern fighters were deployed to the Canary Islands, and the F-5 was the chosen for this role.

Above: An interesting picture of General Rubio and some comrades close to an AIM-9B Sidewinder-armed F-5. The aircraft belonged to the Escuadrón 732 from the Escuela de Reactores.

Right: A close-up of a two seat F-5 (CE.9) from Escuadrón 212. Note the smooth lines of this small but powerful aircraft. The role of the F-5s in the EdA has been, and still is, very important after more than 50 years.

Below: A line up of F-5s (C.9) at Gando AB. Note that, on the front of the aircraft, there is an Ala 46 emblem: a hawk head. All these aircraft shortly after were transferred to Ala 21, but it was necessary to deploy them to the Canary Islands in 1976 with Escuadrón 464.

Above: An AR.9 during a flight. Notice the beautiful profile of the aircraft that was intended to fly both attack and reconnaissance missions.

Left: An F-5 from Ala 21 undergoing maintenance at Morón AB. This aircraft type was the vigilante of the Spanish south flank for many years.

Below: A front view of a CR.9 in tri-tones camouflage pattern. Notice the nose, where the reconnaissance equips were installed. Besides this role, the aircraft was intended to carry out a fighter role too.

Above: A line up of F-5s parked at Son San Juan airport during a deployment of the fighters to the Balearic Islands.

Right: A worn-out F-5 resting at Getafe AB in 1987. The F-5 has showed their endurance and capabilities during more than 50 years within the EdA.

Below: This F-5 in an attack role undergoes maintenance duties at Morón AB.

Chapter 7

McDonnell Douglas F-4C Phantom

History

The 1970s began, and Spain needed a new fighter to replace the battered Sabres and Starfighters. Fortunately, the MAP agreement was renewed in August 1970. It allowed one of the most important aircraft around the world to come to Spain: the Phantom.

The EdA was interested in the F-4E, but budget constraints forced it to accept the F-4C (the other reason for not acquiring the F-4E was that the US did not want to sell F-4Es to Spain). In the end, Spain acquired 36 F-4Cs and three Boeing KC-97Ls (named TK) – one as a strategic tanker aircraft that now Spain needed for fuelling and two C-97s (transport aircraft but only used as replacement source for the KC-97Ls). These Phantoms (referred to as C.12 in the EdA) were not brand new, indeed several were Vietnam veterans and others came from 81st Tactical Fighter Wing from the USAFE (based in Great Britain). All the F-4Cs provided to Spain had been built in 1964 and, of course, required an overhaul before being deployed to the EdA.

The first Spanish Phantom arrived in Spain on 19 February 1971, and the last one in 1972. Once the F-4Cs were in Spain, they were deployed to the Escuadrón 121 'Poker' and Escuadrón 122 'Tenis' from the Ala 12 based at Torrejón AB. The KC-97Ls and C-97Gs were incorporated into this ala too, and Escuadrón 123 was created and dedicated to in-flight refuelling. However, these aircraft only flew for

Undoubtedly, the arrival of the Phantom to Spain in 1971 meant an important improvement in Spanish air power. Thanks to this new fighter, the F-104G could be retired in 1972. In the picture, this C.12, based at Torrejón AB, waits for an upcoming flight.

When in Spanish service, the F-4C Phantom always had the same livery: dark green, green and light brown (the so-called 'lizard scheme'). Note the Ala 12 emblem, a black cat head with the motto 'No le busques tres pies'.

the EdA for three years, and, due to their age, they were retired in 1974–76; with this retirement, the EdA lost the ability to refuel its F-4Cs inflight, therefore drastically reducing their range.

Each escuadrón had 18 aircraft, and these made up the bulk of the Spanish air defences. These aircraft, although older for the USAF, were a crucial acquisition for the EdA thanks to their high-performance and powerful armament (the F-4C carried up to eight missiles, including the medium-range AAM Sparrow that the EdA had recently purchased for the first time).

A Spanish F-4C flies close to two American F-16s (also based at Torrejón, as you can tell by the 'TJ' on the tail). Although the Phantoms that arrived in Spain were 'old warriors', they did their best during the years that they flew for the EdA. Although all the C.12s were ostensibly retired during 1989, the last C.12 (C.12-37) was officially retired in March 1991.

In 1973, all the aircraft at Ala 12 were fully operational, and in 1974, they were sent to be overhauled, where some devices were improved, including the Westinghouse APQ-100 radar and the Litton ASN-48 navigation system.

Very soon, the F-4Cs started to fly in several exercises close to other countries' aircraft, including those of France, Portugal and the US. This aircraft satisfied the EdA; indeed, in 1974, it thought of buying 100 ex-USAF F-4Cs, but this idea never came to fruition.

After several accidents, in 1978, the EdA acquired four used F-4Cs (from the 58th Tactical Fighter Squadron based at Eglin AFB) to replace the written-off Spanish F-4Cs. These four aircraft arrived in Spain (Torrejón) in July/August 1978. In the same purchase, Spain included a reconnaissance version of the Phantom, and four RF-4Cs were acquired (these aircraft came from the 363rd TRW based at Shawn AFB). Also in 1978, the short-range AIM-9B was replaced by the more modern AIM-9J and AIM-9L. Thanks to this weapon improvement, the Phantoms were more powerful still. The Spanish F-4Cs had both fighter and attack capabilities thanks to their weapons payload, high speed and superb manoeuvrability.

In 1978, the FACA Program (Future Combat and Attack Aircraft) was born, which was intended for the purchase of 140 new aircraft (the F-18 was the winner) to replace the F-4Cs and F-5s. Therefore, any thoughts the Spanish government had about improving or buying more F-4s were forgotten.
In spite of this new programme, the Spanish F-4Cs continued to work hard before their replacement arrived. But, in 1986, the newcomers (F-18s) arrived in Zaragoza AB for Ala 15 and, on 28 March 1989, to Torrejón AB for Ala 12, and so the F-4Cs began their last flights within the EdA. During their final

Two Phantoms ready for a scramble rest at one alarm hangar in Torrejón AB, with the full moon observing them. Spain was the last country in the world to retire the F-4C.

years, the shortage of spare parts was increasing, forcing the use of parts from other aircraft as spare parts and diminishing the flyable F-4Cs.

When the EF-18s arrived to Ala 12 on 28 March 1989, two days later all (20) F-4Cs except six were retired (shortly after, one more was retired). So, the five surviving F-4Cs flew together with the RF-4Cs belonging to the Escuadrón 123, but they were not deployed to the reconnaissance escuadrón. The new roles for the surviving F-4Cs were target tug, pilot trainer for RF-4Cs or as a platform to test new weapons, such as various bombs or new missiles from the US. At last, on 11 March 1991, the last F-4Cs were retired. Some of the scrapped F-4Cs were used as ground targets at Las Bárdenas Reales shooting range.

After 69,772 operational service flight hours (across almost 20 years) the superb F-4Cs were retired. Sadly, seven aircraft were lost in accidents, and ten pilots died. But, during these years, the aircraft remained the axis of the Spanish air defence; indeed, the EdA had the honour to be the last air force in the world to retire the F-4Cs. Perhaps it had not been the Phantom the EdA desired, but, once they arrived in Spain, there was no doubt that the F-4Cs were what the EdA needed to continue growing. Although they were retired from service in 1991, the Spanish story of the Phantom had not ended.

F-4C Performance

Service Time in Spain	1971–91
General Characteristics	
Wingspan	11.71m (38ft 5in)
Length	18.47m (60ft 6in)
Height	5.03m (16ft 6in)
Wing area	49.23m² (530sq ft)
Weight	
Empty	12,823kg (28,270lb)
Max take-off	26,303kg (57,988lb)
Engine	2 x General Electric J79-GE-15
Other	
Maximum speed	2,548km/h (1,583mph) at 14,721m
Operative service ceiling	18,104m (59,396ft)
Combat range with fuel tanks	3,700km (2,299 miles)
Armament	
Inner	No
Hardpoints	4 for AIM-9L Sidewinder AAM 4 for AIM-7E Sparrow III Bombs, rockets or cannon (20mm M-61 Vulcan up to 7,500kg/16,535lb)

Liveries

The camouflage of the Spanish F-4Cs was the typical standard of Southeast Asia (left from the USAF's involvement in Vietnam), with small national insignias. The upper surfaces were painted medium green, dark green and dark tan, while the under surfaces were painted in light grey. The radome was coated in black.

Unit and aircraft numbers were added in black paint. National roundels were in six positions, with the St. Andrew's Cross in the tail. It was a typical feature of the Phantoms to have a large Ala 12 emblem consisting of a cat's head with the motto 'No le busques tres pies' ('Do not split hairs') painted on the fin. Both Escuadrón 121 and Escuadrón 122 bared this emblem.

When a F-4C is taking off, everybody can hear its roaring. This aircraft from Ala 12 was replaced in Spain with the F/A-18A Hornet. All the F-4Cs were either deployed to the Escuadrón 121 'Poker' (as was the aircraft in the picture) or Escuadrón 122 from Ala 12.

This Phantom is a good example to understand the UNs painted on Spanish aircraft: 122: the first number identifies the unit that the aircraft belongs to (Escuadrón 122); 15: the aircraft order number into its unit, though this is not necessarily chronological to when the aircraft was purchased.

This picture allows us to see the massive profile of the Phantom. Notice that there are at least 5 F-4Cs from Escuadrón 122 parked at this Torrejón's airstrip.

A F-4C almost ready for take-off. This aircraft belonged to Escuadrón 121. Also, note the now smaller St. Andrew's Cross on the tail, which was used on the Spanish F-4Cs to limit their visibility and recognisability.

This F-4C is one of the guest stars in this Open Gates Exhibition at Torrejón. At that time, there were no fences between the public and the aircraft. The picture was taken in June 1973.

Above: This rear view of a F-4C allows us to see the Ala 12 emblem, consisting of a cat's head with the motto 'No le busques tres pies' painted on the fin. Notice that is not a low-visibility emblem.

Left: Honouring their name, like two phantoms a couple of F-4Cs fly quickly to their destination. Notice the typical standard Southeast Asia camouflage scheme used by the Spanish Phantoms.

Chapter 8
Mirage F-1

History

At last, thanks to the arrival of the Mirage IIIs and the Mc Donnell Douglas F-4C, Spain had an air force able to defend the Spanish skies like never before. But the EdA wanted to include a new fighter and settled on the French Mirage F-1 and purchased 15 F-1Cs in 1972. These aircraft would be deployed to Escuadrón 141 'Chico' ('Boy'); from Ala 14 bases in Los llanos. The unit was created in June 1974, shortly before the arrival of the aircraft). This escuadrón became operational when the first 4 F-1CEs arrived on 18 June 1975. On 13 November 1979, a second squadron was created within Ala 14, Escuadrón 142 'Dardo' ('Dart'), which was equipped with F-1s too. The main role of the Mirages in both escuadrones was primarily all-weather fighter and secondarily attack fighter-bomber.

Between June 1975 and April 1983, the EdA received 73 Mirage F-1s in three batches. Regardless of the aircraft type and any improvements made, the Spanish F-1s were named C.14 (single-seater) and CE.14 (two-seater) but the aircraft were of three different types: the 45 F-1CEs ('E' for España) were called C.14A, the six F-1BEs (two-seaters) were called CE.14A and the 22 F-1EEs were called C.14B. The main role of the F-1 was air defence, and thanks to the many aircraft purchased, the EdA could set up two units: Escuadrón 141 and Escuadrón 462.

The superb performance of the aircraft allowed an aerobatic patrol (Patrulla Acrobática del Ala 14) to be created between 1978 and 1990. At the beginning, this aerobatic team flew only four aircraft, but this was soon increased to six aircraft, all manned by Ala 14's pilots.

The F-1EEs were fitted with a non-removable refuelling probe to the right of the cockpit, which was a crucial device for those aircraft operating in the Canary Islands. Subsequently, all the F-1EEs were deployed to Escuadrón 462 with Ala 46 at Gando AB. Before the arrival of the F-1EEs to Gando, several F-1CEs from Ala 14 were deployed temporarily to Gando. Escuadrón 462 also received two two-seater F-1BEs. The first six aircraft arrived at Gando AB on 8 March 1982; four days later, Escuadrón 464 (with F-5s) was disbanded and Escuadrón 462 was activated (with 22 F-1EEs and two

In 2002, the EdA took part in the *Red Flag* exercise with Mirage F-1Ms from Ala 14. This Mirage F-1M is being refuelled when flying to Alaska. The in-flight refuelling probe was typical of the 22 F-1EEs (single seat) and two F-1BEs (two-seat) that the EdA purchased to deploy them to Escuadrón 462, based in Gando AB. They were delivered between February 1982 and April 1983. Notice that, under the front part of the aircraft, a fake canopy has been painted to trick the enemy.

F-1BE). These aircraft became the defenders of the Canary Islands for many years. The performance of the F-1s, together with the in-flight refuelling probe, made these aircraft suitable for this mission. The F-1s operated in the Canary Islands until 2002, when the Hornets replaced them.

The other significant unit where the F-1 operated was with Ala 11, based at Manises. On 1 October 1992, the unit's Mirage IIIs were retired and replaced temporarily by the Mirage F-1s from Ala 14. The first six F-1s arrived the same day and were deployed to Escuadrón 111. The Mirage III's pilots were posted to Escuadrón 142 (which acted as a conversion unit this time) to be trained in the F-1 in order to come back to Ala 11. Another unit where the F-1s were attached from time to time was the CLAEX (a tester and experimental unit), where they tested new weapons and modifications.

Due to both the impressive performance of the F-1s and also the high levels of attrition caused by several accidents, the Spanish government purchased new F-1s in the 1990s. Five ex-Armeé de l'Air F-1s were purchased (one two-seater and four F-1CEs) and were delivered between November 1994 and March 1995. The other F-1 source was Qatar, as 13 aircraft had been purchased (11 single-seater F-1DDAs and two two-seater F-1EDAs) and delivered between August 1994 and January 1998. The EdA renamed these aircraft C.14C and CE.14C, respectively. Surprisingly, those aircraft from the latter source were retired from 2002, primarily because the systems of the aircraft purchased from Qatar were not compatible with the other Spanish F-1 systems.

In the mid-1990s, the F-1s were getting old, and a new aircraft was needed. This desired option was the Eurofighter, but this would take a long time to be manufactured, so an interim solution was required. This was the improvement of all the Spanish F-1s, which was authorised in June 1995. Therefore, 55 aircraft entered the modernisation programme (although two were lost in accidents), but C.14Cs and CE.14Cs were excluded. The improvements works were made in two places: 26 single-seater and three two-seaters were sent to SABCA facilities in Gosseliers (Belgium), while 23 single-seaters and one two-seater were improved in Spain (in Albacete). After improvement, the aircraft were renamed F-1Ms and featured better avionics, HOTAS (hands on throttle and stick), HUDs, the capability to

The EdA was very satisfied with the F-1s, so it decided to purchase some more used F-1s. It purchased ten F-1EDAs and two F-1DDAs from the Qatar Emiri Air Force, which were delivered in 1994–1997. At the beginning, the aircraft kept their two-toned livery, but they were later painted in grey.

employ the AIM-9 JULI missile and many other new improvements intended to lengthen the service life of the F-1s until 2010–15. While the aircraft were being modernised, Spain had less F-1s in service, and Ala 14 had to take away the 'alarm section' that the F-1s carried out. This scarcity was partially solved thanks to the new F-1s purchased to Qatar, which, as mentioned, were not involved in the improvement plan.

The F-1s took part in many international NATO exercises and collaborations throughout their service. For example, four Spanish F-1Ms from Ala 14 were sent to Siauliai AB (Lithuania) in 2006 as part of NATO's Baltic air policing initiative. Later, other aircraft including F-18s and Eurofighters would be sent to the Baltic Countries in similar roles.

In 2013, the F-1Ms were retired definitively from the EdA, although the number of operational F-1Ms had been shrinking for many years. During all the years (37) that the F-1s operated within the EdA, they achieved more than 254,790 operational service flight hours: mainly in Ala 14 (200,000hrs), then Ala 46 (46,960hrs), Ala 11 (6,380hrs) and CLAEX (1,450hrs). Sadly, during these years, 35 aircraft were lost in accidents and 14 pilots died. After the F-86, the F-1 is the aircraft with the highest rate of accidents within the EdA, despite its excellent performance overall.

The Spanish government tried to sell several F-1Ms to Argentina, but this never came to fruition. At last, in 2017, Draken International purchased 22 F-1Ms in order to use them as attackers and aggressors for the training of several air forces around the world. In total, the number of F-1s that flew with the Spanish cockades was 91, and although they were retired from service, they are still remembered with warm nostalgia because of their good work in Spain.

When the first F-1s arrived in Spain, they were painted in a 'lizard scheme'. This picture shows aircraft from Ala 14 lined-up at Son San Juan airport in November 1981.

F-1C Performance

Service Time in Spain	1975–2013
General Characteristics	
Wingspan	8.40m (27ft 7in)
Length	15.23m (50ft)
Height	4.50m (14ft 8in)
Wing area	25m² (269sq ft)
Weight	
Empty	11,200kg (24,692lb)
Max take-off	16,200kg (35,715lb)
Engine	1 x SNECMA Atar 9K-50
Other	
Maximum speed	2,695km/h (1,675mph)
Operative service ceiling	20,000m (65,617ft)
Combat range with fuel tanks	4,000km (2,486 miles)
Armament	
Inner	2 x DEFA 553 30mm cannon (125rpg)
Hardpoints	5 + 2 wingtips up to: 2 x AIM-9 Sidewinder AAM 2 x R.550 Magic 2 x Matra Super R.530 Bombs (up to 5,200kg/11,464lb) 3 x fuel tanks

As time went by, the Spanish F-1s replaced their lizard livery with NATO light grey. In this picture, three F-1Ms from Ala 14 are flying over La Mancha (a region near Los Llanos AB). Note the low-visibility St. Andrew's Cross and Ala 14 emblem. Although it cannot be seen in the picture, under the front part of the aircraft was a fake painted canopy.

Liveries

The different liveries that the Spanish F-1s used are very interesting. The 45 F-1CEs and six F-1BEs had the upper surfaces in a tri-coloured scheme (sand, green, brown), while the under surfaces were painted in light grey. The radome was in black.

The 22 F-1EEs were deployed to Gando AB and it was necessary to choose a paint that would protect the aircraft from the hot and wet climate. Therefore, they were painted in a medium blue on the upper surfaces and light grey on the under surfaces, similar to the Armeé del l'Air painting scheme used in the F-1s. The radome was in black.

When the ex-Qatari aircraft arrived in Spain, they kept their two-tone (sand and brown) livery but were later repainted in light grey. From the late 1980s to the beginning of the '90s, the EdA ordered that all the aircraft had to be painted in light grey, so all the surviving F-1s were repainted in this way. Even the radomes, which had until this point been black, were painted in grey too. It was typical that the F-1s painted in light grey had a false canopy painted on the under surface of the cockpit, in an attempt to confuse the enemy as to whether the aircraft was up or down.

The identifying letters and numbers were painted in black, and of course the national roundels were in six positions with the St. Andrew's Cross on the tail (on the top of the rudder) in low-visibility markings. At the beginning, the cross was over a white background, but later it was painted over the aircraft's camouflage. When all the aircraft were painted in grey, the cross was in dark grey over a light grey background.

The unit emblems have always been painted on the engine nacelles; at the beginning in a colourful pattern, then in a low-visibility one (two colours).

In the mid-90s, the F-1 was modernised, so 51 single-seaters and four two-seaters were upgraded to 'M' standard. Here we see the standard look of a Mirage F-1 during its last years flying for the EdA, complete with light grey livery, low-visibility emblem and St. Andrew's Cross. Note the chaff/flare dispenser above the ventral fin. This aircraft was one of the four F-1Ms sent to Lithuania in 2006.

Left: A former F-1EE from Escuadrón 462 became an F-1M from Ala 14, which we can tell thanks to the emblem painted on the engine nacelle. The in-flight refuelling probe was typical of the 22 F-1EEs delivered to Escuadrón 462 in 1981–1983. Notice the radome painted in grey.

Below: A beautiful picture of a F-1EE from Escuadrón 462 at Gando. This aircraft is easily recognisable thanks to the in-flight refuelling probe, the typical blue scheme on the upper surfaces and the hawk emblem painted on the engine nacelle. Notice the unit number 46 (from the Ala) and not 462 (from the Escuadrón) and the wide main landing gear.

Five of the six aircraft belonging to the Patrulla Acrobática del Ala 14. Notice that they have the early Ala 14 painting scheme. The F-1 showed itself to be a very powerful aircraft for aerobatics.

Above: A close-up of two of the aircraft from Patrulla Acrobática del Ala 14 in 'lizard scheme'. The Patrulla only lasted 12 years because of the creation of the Patrulla Águila. The aircraft are flying over Los Llanos AB.

Right: This aircraft from Escuadrón 462 shows us the smooth and sharp profile of this aircraft as well as the surprisingly small size of the cockpit. The aircraft from this unit were very similar in painting scheme to the French Mirage F-1s.

A close-up of the armament carried by this Mirage F-1M (before being upgraded to a F-1EE). We can see two Sidewinder missiles and three bombs, but more weapons are concealed. Although the main F-1 role was air defence (all-weather fighter), they were a good fighter-bomber too.

A close-up of one of the two F-1EDAs purchased from Qatar. Notice the two-tone camouflage schemes and Ala 11's emblem painted on the engine nacelle. The ex-Qatar aircraft were not upgraded to F-1M standard.

This F-1CE has the typical livery used for these aircraft during their first years within the EdA; upper surfaces in a tri-coloured scheme (sand, green, brown). Perhaps one of the most beautiful painting schemes ever used within the EdA.

Above: A F-1CE from Ala 14, with its typical tri-tone painting scheme during a visit to Mallorca. Notice the colourful emblem painted on the engine nacelle. Later, this emblem was replaced by a two-toned one in low-visibility pattern.

Right: A close-up of the false canopy usually painted on the under surface of the cockpit in the F-1s. Notice that, from long distances, the trick was very convincing. This aircraft is now the static guard of the Tablada barracks in Seville, belonging to the EdA. (Eduardo M. Gil Martínez)

Above: The Canary Islands were well protected by the F-1s from Escuadrón 462. This one bears the typical camouflage pattern of this unit; medium blue on the upper surfaces and light grey on the under surfaces.

Left: A Mirage F-1 from Ala 14, showing a light grey livery typical of the last years of its time in the EdA.

Below: This image of a Mirage F-1C shows off the landing gear and the beautiful livery.

Chapter 9

Harrier AV-8S

History

Some combat jets were operated both by the EdA and the Armada Española (Spanish Navy); the most famous being the legendary Harrier. The US-Spain agreement meant that, on 20 December 1967, the US Navy assigned the light aircraft carrier USS *Cabot* to Spain, which the Armada renamed *Dédalo* (the Armada had another aircraft carrier during the 1920s with the same name). As Spain had no suitable aircraft, the ship was considered as a helicopter carrier. Shortly after, in 1973, the Armada considered that *Dédalo* could be converted to be an aircraft carrier, if it managed to purchase suitable aircraft for this ship.

The aircraft chosen was the very innovative Harrier; with its V/STOL (vertical/short takeoff and landing) capabilities, it was perfect for use on an aircraft carrier such as the *Dédalo*. The Spanish government approved a demonstration of the aircraft on the *Dédalo* in 1972. The test was carried out by a RAF GR.1 Harrier on 8 November 1972 in Barcelona waters, and it was a great success (despite the risk of the aircraft engines burning the *Dédalo*'s wooden deck). Shortly after, the Spanish government tried to purchase eight Harriers from the United Kingdom. But the political relationship between Spain and United Kingdom (and thus the Hawker Siddeley manufacturer) was not good, so the acquisition was rejected. Spain at last managed to purchase them from the US, from the other Harrier manufacturer in the world: McDonnell Douglas. In July 1973, the government ordered six AV-8As (single-seater) and two TAV-8As (two-seater), although the original plan was to purchase 25 aircraft. The aircraft destined for Spain were nicknamed 'Matador' by the manufacturer, but this name did not catch on in Spain. They were also given the letter 'S' in their registrations to differentiate them from the type 'A' aircraft used by the US marines.

In 1976, the changes to the *Dédalo*'s deck started. It was reinforced in order to safely carry and deploy the Harrier on board, and metal sheathing was laid down on the rear of the deck. Ten Navy helicopters pilots (five SH-3s and five AB-204Ds) were sent to the US (Pensacola) for a six-month training course to fly the Harrier. They flew Beech T-34Cs and TA-4Js before being moved on to Spanish AV-8As. Sadly, one Spanish Harrier crashed during the training period. When the training finished, the *Dédalo* shipped to Mayport in order to bring the seven surviving aircraft to Spain. On 4 September 1976, a unit, Escuadrilla 8ª, was created for the Harriers.

At last, in March 1977, Escuadrilla 8ª was operational, with five AV-8Ss and two TAV-8Ss. The official Armada Española name for these aircraft was VA-1 for the AV-8S and VAE-1 for the TAV-8Ss. In 1977, a new group of pilots was sent to the US for training, and the next group of pilots were trained at Rota NAV, another Harrier base.

A flamboyant AV/8S landing vertically on the *Dédalo*'s deck. This small aircraft allowed the Armada Española to increase its operational range. Notice the fuel tanks under the wings and the large Spanish cockades.

In 1980, five new aircraft were purchased (all AV-8Ss) and were delivered in June 1980. These aircraft were similar to those seven mentioned before. The main difference was an improved VHF radio device.

The primary roles of these aircraft were close air support and attack, air defence, air reconnaissance and air superiority. But their short range was a problem, so from 1985 all the single-seater aircraft were fitted with a removable refuelling probe over the port engine nacelle. Thanks to this improvement, the range was increased, and the first in-flight refuelling took place on 19 September 1985.

The aircraft were fitted with several devices, including a gyrocompass, TACAN, IFF/SIF, and AN/ALE 7 electronic countermeasures, and a 16mm camera and 70mm F95 camera.

Meanwhile, Spain was building a new aircraft carrier (*Príncipe de Asturias*) in order to replace the venerable *Dédalo*. This new vessel was fitted with a ski-jump ramp, and Spanish Harriers were sent to the United Kingdom for training at Yeovilton Royal Navy Air Base. The arrival of the new aircraft carrier in 1989 also meant the arrival of a new and improved Harrier in Spain: the AV-8B 'Harrier II'.

Then, with the arrival of the Harrier IIs, and the EdA decided to sell the nine surviving TAV/AV-8Ss to Thailand in 1993. The last flight of a Spanish AV-8S took place on 21 October 1996 and Escuadrilla 8ª was disbanded on 24 October 1996. As the aircraft were American-made, this sale required US approval to go ahead, and this was not given until 1995.

The sale agreement was signed on 10 November 1996. On 1 July 1997, the Thai aircraft carrier (made in Spain by Empresa Nacional Bazán de Construcciones Navales), with those Harriers now in Thai markings, set sail to Thailand from Rota NAS after being refurbished by CASA.

After almost 20 service years, the Harriers had achieved 26,244 operational service flight hours and had been flown by approximately 70 naval pilots. During their service time with the Armada Española, three Harriers were lost in accidents, killing one pilot. Additionally, when training in the US, another Spanish Harrier was lost in 1976 before being assigned to the Armada Española.

This lower view of the AV-8S allow us to see the bright white under surfaces where the large black unit number and the word 'ARMADA' stand out. The Spanish Harrier never tried to hide nor to be discreet.

AV-8S/TAV-8S Performance

Service Time in Spain	1977–96
General Characteristics	
Wingspan	9.45m (31ft)
Length	14.0m (46ft); 17.20m (56ft 5in) TAV-8S
Height	3.30m (10ft 9in); 4.17m (13ft 7in) TAV-8S
Wing area	21.37m² (230sq ft)
Weight	
Empty	5,400kg (11,905lb); 6,014kg (13,259lb) TAV-8S
Max take-off	10,900kg (24,030lb)
Engine	1 x Rolls-Royce Pegasus F402-RR-402B
Other	
Maximum speed	1,176km/h (731mph)
Operative service ceiling	15,240m (50,000ft)
Combat range with fuel tanks	3,000km (1,864 miles)
Armament	
Inner	No
Hardpoints	1 central and 4 under the wings intended for up to: 4 x AIM-9P/L Sidewinder AAM 4 x 127mm ZUNI rocket launchers 5 x 225kg bombs 2 x 30mm ADEN cannons

Liveries

The livery of the Spanish AV-8S was always the same; all the upper surfaces and sides were painted in bright light grey and the under surfaces were painted bright white.

Large Spanish cockades were placed in six positions, the aircraft number was on the tail and the unit number on the engine nacelles. From 1976 to 1980, the registration number was 008-XXX, but from 1980 until 1996 it became 01-8XX (from 801 to 814). This number was painted on the left upper wing, while on the right upper wing the word 'MARINA' was painted in black until 1980, and from 1980, it was the word 'ARMADA'. The reason was that, from January 1980, the Spanish Navy changed its name from Marina de Guerra to Armada Española. Similarly, on the port under wing the word 'MARINA' was painted (later 'ARMADA') and the aircraft number was painted on the starboard under wing.

The aircraft number was painted on the fin too, either on top of the fin (from 1976 to 1980) or the lower part of the fin (1980 until 1996). The word 'MARINA' was also painted in black on the rear fuselage, replaced from 1980 by 'ARMADA'. An anchor over a wing was painted on the tail's bottom, as was typical for Spanish navy aircraft.

Above: A stunning picture of a beautiful and very special aircraft. Notice the straight separation line between the white (under surfaces) and the light grey (upper surfaces) on the aircraft. Behind the AV-8S, two T-33s are parked.

Left: A couple of AV-8S flying over aircraft carrier *Dédalo*. We know the picture was taken after 1980, because the word 'ARMADA' is painted on the rear fuselage. Note Escuadrilla 8ª's emblem painted below the front part of the cockpit and the anchor over a wing painted on the tail. (Public Domain by Lieutenant Commander John Leenhouts, US Navy)

Three AV-8Ss (two in Spanish markings and one in Thai markings) and a TAV-8S (in Thai markings) are lined up at Zaragoza AB ready for a training sortie at Las Bárdenas Reales shooting range. This picture was taken shortly before all the Spanish 'Harriers' were painted with Thai markings. The TAV-8S still has the Spanish paint scheme, while the fourth aircraft (a Thai AV-8S) has been painted in a new grey scheme with black radome.

Not always, but often, Escuadrilla 8ª's emblem was painted on the front part of the cockpit. It consisted of a crossed chain and an eagle holding an anchor with the motto 'Per Aspera Ad Astra' ('Through the difficulties toward the stars'). As this aircraft belonged to the Armada rather than the EdA, the St. Andrew's Cross was not used.

A beautiful rear view of an ex-Spanish TAV-8S (within the Royal Thai Navy this aircraft has the serial 3101, but previously carried the number 01-807), now in Royal Thai Navy markings. These aircraft played an important role for the training of new pilots, and not just those from Spain; indeed, Italian pilots from the Marina Militare (Italian Navy) were trained in 1990 in the Spanish two-seater Harriers.

Above: This picture was taken before the change in name of the Spanish Navy in 1980 (on 1 May 1977). Notice the word 'MARINA' painted on the rear fuselage. Furthermore, the unit number is still 008, which was was replaced in 1980 by 01-8XX. (Public Domain by James Bishop)

Right: An AV-8S during a stationary flight. The V/STOL capability of the Harrier was necessary in order to operate the aircraft from the *Dédalo*. This aircraft was the first jet used by the Armada Española, followed by the AV-8B several years after. Notice the open airbrake.

Above: This picture of a TAV-8A shows the clear separation between the grey (upper surfaces) and the white (under surfaces) on this aircraft type. The aircraft is bearing the unit numbers used from 1980 until 1996, 01-8XX. The aircraft number ('7') is painted on the lower part of the fin.

Left: This image shows one of the two TAV-8Ss that the Armada Española purchased in 1973 and received in 1976 as it rests at Rota NAS. This two-seater aircraft type was necessary for training future Harrier pilots.

Below: This TAV-8A is parked at Rota NAS and bears the unit number used from 1976 to 1980, this time the number '7'. The same number is repeated at the top of the fin and on the port upper wing and on the starboard under wing.

Above: The same TAV-8A in a lateral view. This aircraft enabled the armada to maintain a small but effective task force wherever needed.

Right: A close-up of the rear part of a TAV-8A. Note the typical wing arrangement useful for attack missions.

Below: A close-up of the front part of a TAV-8A (008-08). Again, note the agile lines of this superb aircraft.

A former Spanish Harrier, now belonging to the Royal Thai Navy, armed with small bombs. After several years of successful service, the Harriers began a new life in other parts of the world.

Another former Spanish Harrier now belonging to the Royal Thai Navy, although this time is a two seat TAV-8A.

Chapter 10
EdA Structure and Radio Codenames

The basic unit within the EdA is called an ala (wing). Each Ala has between one and three escuadrones (squadrons), but most commonly it will have two. When there is a third escuadrón, it is often used as a conversion unit for the training of new pilots for new aircraft. Most of the time, the escuadrón's number begins with the Ala's number, so within Ala 11, there are three escuadrones numbered 111, 112 and 113, and within Ala 14 there are the 141 and 142 escuadrones. There have also been units that were similar to, but not considered, alas – these were named Grupos, and they could be attached to various alas. For example, in 1989, Ala 15 was renamed Group 15 and was attached to Ala 31, together with Group 31. This was a temporary name.

The number of aircraft in each escuadrón has differed during the last 75 years, but it is normally between 18 and 24 aircraft. Therefore, the number of aircraft in one ala is usually between 36 and 48. However, these numbers can differ for various types of wings. As an example, Ala 11 (a fighter wing) nowadays has 38 aircraft (Eurofighter EF2000) divided between two Escuadrones: 111 and 113; and the Ala 31 (a transport Wing) only has 14 A400Ms in service.

On occasion, an escuadrón does not belong to an ala. For example, Escuadrón 104 (F-104G) was an independent unit from November 1967 to May 1972, although it was eventually absorbed into Ala 12 with the same name. In addition to alas and escuadrones, there are other minor units called escuadrillas. Usually, these units did not belong to a major unit and were independent.

Although we have mentioned the radio codename of several escuadrones in the text, a complete list is compiled below.

Escuadrón	Radio Codename
211	Gallo (Cock)
212	Sisón (Bird)
122	Tenis (Tennis)
123	Titán (Titan)
231	Patas Negras (Black Legs)
232	Mago (Wizard)
151	Toro (Bull)
153	Ebro (a Spanish river)
154	Marte (Mars)
141	Chico (Boy)
142	Dardo (Dart)
121	Póker (Poker)
111	Dólar (Dollar)
462	Halcón (Hawk)

Spanish Military Jets 1954–2022

A table of the aircraft assigned to each ala/grupo

	Ala 1	Ala 2	Ala 3	Ala 4	Ala 5	Ala 6	Ala 10	Ala 11	Ala 12	Ala 14	Ala 15	Ala 16	Ala 21	Ala 23	Ala 41	Ala 43	Ala 46	8ª EA	9ª EA	Grupo/Ala 41	Ala 74
T-33	■	■	■	■	■	■															
F-86	■	■	■	■	■	■			■		■										
Ha-200/220								■			■		■				■				
F-104									■												
Mirage III							■	■													
F-5										■			■	■			■				
F-4/RF-4								■	■	■											
F-1								■		■							■				
AV-8A																		■			
C-101											■	■		■						■	■
F-18									■		■						■				
AV-8B																			■		
E-2000										■											

List of jets and their Spanish names

Aircraft	Spanish Name	1954–1978	1978–Present
North American F-86F	Sabre	C.5	
North American T-6D	Sabre	C.6	AE.6
Lockheed F-104G		C.8	
Lockheed TF-104G		CE.8	
CASA Northrop F-5A		C.9	A.9
CASA Northrop RF-5A		CR.9	AR.9
CASA Northrop F-5B		CE.9	AE.9
Hispano HA-200A	Saeta	C.10A	A.10A
Hispano HA-200D	Saeta	C.10B	A.10B
Hispano HA-220	Súper Saeta	C.10C	A.10C
Dassault Mirage III EE	Plancheta		C.11
Dassault Mirage III DE	Plancheta		CE.11
McDonnell F-4C			C.12
McDonnell RF-4C			CR.12
Mirage F-1 (single seat)			C.14
Mirage F-1 (two-seat)			CE.14
C-101EB	Mirlo (Blackbird)		E.25
McDonnell EF-18A			C.15
McDonnell EF-18B			CE.15
Eurofighter EFA-2000A	Tifón (Typhoon)		C.16
Eurofighter EFA-2000B	Tifón		CE.16
AV-8A	Matador/Harrier		VA-1
TAV-8A (two-seat)	Matador/Harrier		VAE-1
AV-8B			VA.1A
TAV-8B (two-seat)			VA.1B

Glossary

Academia General del Aire	Air General Academy
Ala/Alas	Wing/Wings
Ala de Caza	Fighter Wing
CASA	Construcciones Aeronáuticas Sociedad Anónima, aeronautical manufacturer, now owned by Airbus
CLAEX	Centro Logistico de Armamento y Experimentación (Logistic Centre for Armament and Experimentation)
Destacamento	Detachment
Ejército del Aire (EdA)	Spanish Air Force
Escuadrón (Escuadrones)	Squadron (Squadrons). Usually, the squadrons are named 'Number + Escuadrón' (141 Escuadrón), but in the text we use 'Escuadrón + number', (Escuadrón 141)
Escuela de Reactores	Jet Training School
Mando	Command
Patrulla	Patrol
Número de Unidad	Unit Number (UN)

Bibliography

Gil Martínez, Eduardo Manuel and Arráez Cerdá, Juan, *Spanish Air Force Aircraft: 1939–2021*, Key Publishing (2021)
González Serrano, José Luis, *Las unidades y el material del Ejército del Aire durante la Segunda Guerra mundial*, AF Editores (2005)
González Serrano, José Luis, 'Recopilación números de tipo y denominaciones oficiales de los aviones del Ejército del Aire (1939–2012)'
Ministerio de Defensa, *Aviones militares españoles* (1986)
Paloque, Gérard, *Aerobatics Teams: Histoire and Collections* (2010)
Paloque, Gérard, *Aeronautiques Navales du Monde*, Heimdal, (2021)
Paloque, Gérard, *Avions de combat de L'OTAN*, Heimdal (2020)
Pecker, Beatriz and Pérez, Carlos, *Crónica de la aviación española*, Silex (1983)
Alas Españolas. Reserva anticipada ediciones, full collection 1999–2004
Magazine Avion Revue, Key Publishing España, 2019–2021, several articles
Magazine Defensa, several articles.

Other books you might like:

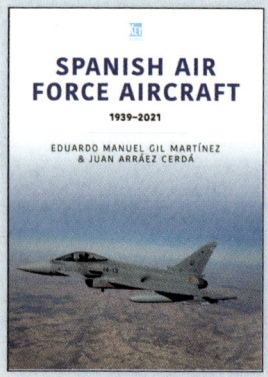
Air Forces Series, Vol. 3

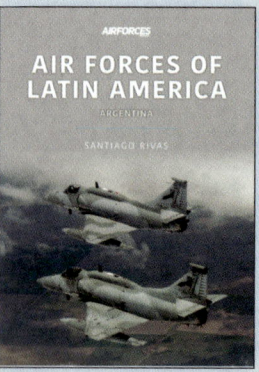
Air Forces Series, Vol. 1

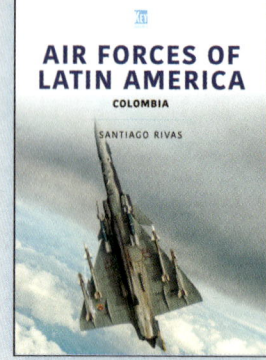
Air Forces Series, Vol. 5

Modern Military Aircraft Series, Vol. 3

Modern Military Aircraft Series, Vol. 5

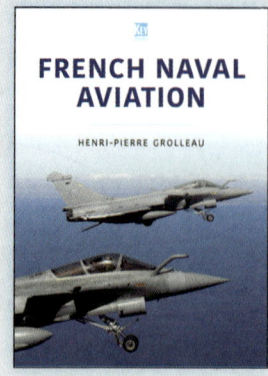
Modern Military Aircraft Series, Vol. 7

For our full range of titles please visit:
shop.keypublishing.com/books

VIP Book Club

Sign up today and receive
TWO FREE E-BOOKS

Be the first to find out about our forthcoming book releases and receive exclusive offers.

Register now at **keypublishing.com/vip-book-club**

Our VIP Book Club is a 100% spam-free zone, and we will never share your email with anyone else. You can read our full privacy policy at: privacy.keypublishing.com